Walking and Exploring the

Northern Broads

By Joe Jackson

First Edition

All maps provided are OS OpenData with additions. It is recommended to take a detailed up-to-date map of the area with you whilst on a walk. Public Footpaths are generally well waymarked but there are areas which may require some basic map reading skills.

For walks and video guides for hundreds of routes all over Great Britain then visit:

www.walkinginthewild.co.uk

Broads National Park logo used with kind permission of the Broads Authority.

While every effort is made by myself to ensure the accuracy of this guidebook before going to print, changes can occur during the lifetime of an edition. It is recommended that you check local information like public transport, shops and accommodation if any of these will be required prior to starting any walk or holiday. Even rights of way can be altered over time.

Please keep to the countryside code by being safe, plan ahead and follow any signs. Leave gates and property as you find them. Protect plants and animals by taking litter home. Keep dogs under close control and please be considerate to other people.

Front Cover: Brograve Drainage Mill (Walk 16)

Contents

The Broads National Park

An overview of England's most important wetland

The Broads National Park is formed of a series of mostly navigable rivers and lakes (known as Broads) that together, with the surrounding marshland, create the largest protected wetland in the country. Home to dozens of very rare species of wildlife including Bittern, Crane, Bearded Tit and the Swallowtail Butterfly, there are numerous nature reserves to explore within the national park boundary. Within its 117 square miles there are also three long distance trails as well as countless miles of marsh and riverbank walking. The Broads were formed from peat excavations in the middle ages and as sea levels began to rise these diggings became flooded, and now many hundreds of years later provide the delicate habitat we see today.

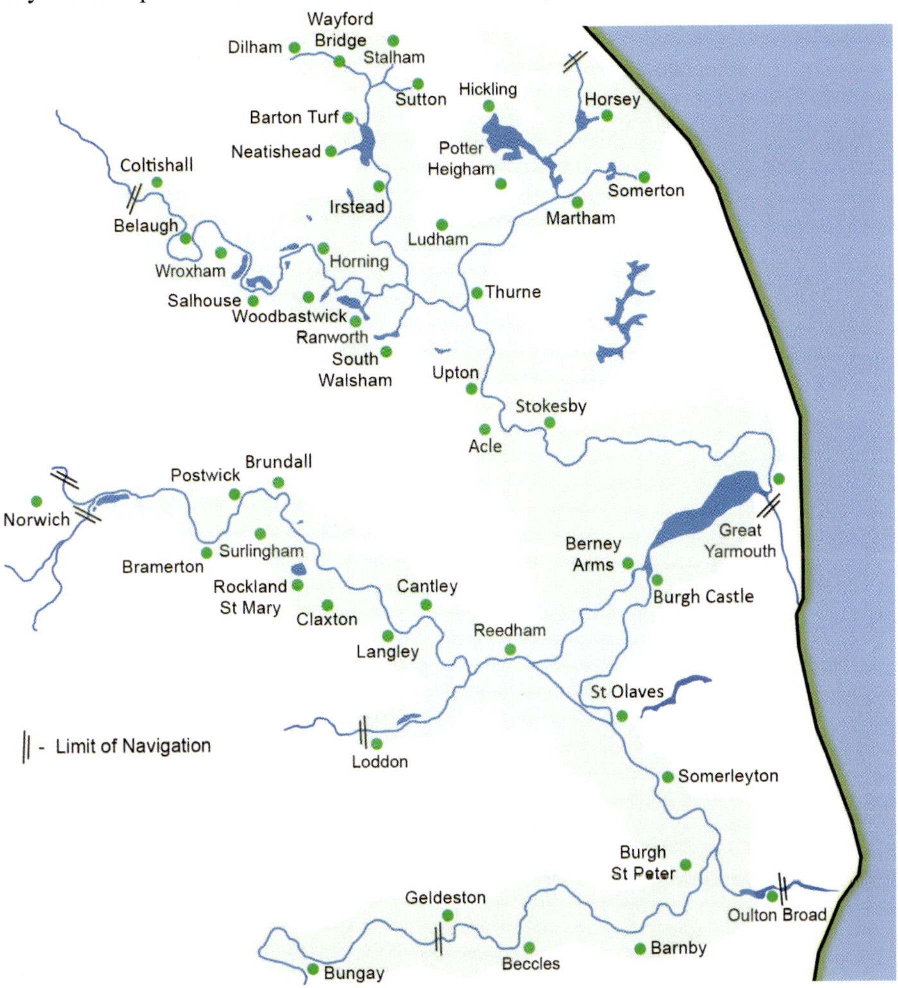

Understanding the Maps and Icons

At the start of each chapter are a selection of icons at the bottom of the page which allow for a brief overview of what is offered at the town or village. These icons indicate the following:

Convenience Store | Mooring | Pub | Eatery | Pharmacy | Nature Reserve | Historic Interest

The maps included in this book are provided by Ordnance Survey OpenData VectorMap® with additions that most visitors may find useful such as footpaths, pubs and restaurants, public transport links, points of interest, parking and mooring. Please be aware that some places may charge for moorings (especially outside public houses) but this is sometimes offset if you are using their services. Signs should be in place stating the charge or whether it is 24 hour free mooring. Car Parking is also included on the map as a blue 'P' of which there may be a small charge. Boatyards have also been added to aid pleasure cruisers to additional facilities such as pump outs and drinking water.

Public Footpaths

Public House

Point of Interest

Moorings

Train Station

Bridge (With Height)

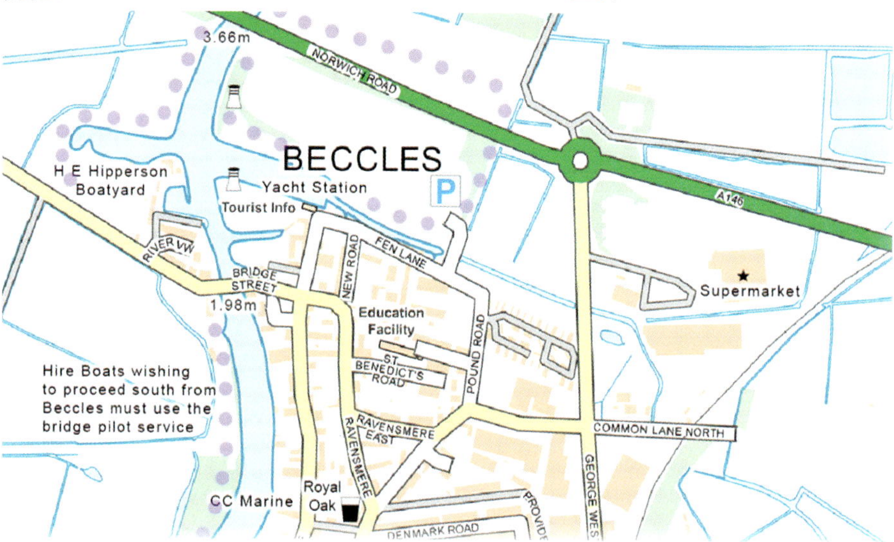

Holidaying on the Broads

The Broads National Park is most famous for being a holiday destination for boat enthusiasts with over 200km (120 miles) of navigable waterways. The seven main rivers within the national park are the River Waveney, Thurne, Bure, Chet, Yare, Ant and Wensum which connect together along with 63 broads (lakes) to form one of the largest wetlands in the UK. Naturally with all this water around most visitors choose to take in the sights from the river and either book a fully equipped motor cruiser or yacht. To see the entire area a minimum of one week is recommended due to tidal restrictions at Breydon Water which can prevent access to the southern or northern broads and rivers. Holidaying on the Broads has been around for decades with many well established marinas offering various craft for hire and have been around for nearly 100 years! Whether it be a back to basics type of holiday or state of the art luxury cruiser, there's something for every budget and taste. For those who want to take things a little slower then seeing areas of the Broads from the adventurous position of a Kayak or Canoe is highly recommended, accessing areas other boaters cannot reach and being at one with the river and wildlife. If sailing the rivers is not for you then there are plenty of B&Bs, Caravan and Campsites and riverside cottages dotted around the Broads providing the perfect base to venture out on foot or bicycle. There are literally hundreds of miles of footpath and bridleways in and around the Broads National Park taking walkers to hidden viewpoints and wildlife hot-spots that simply cannot be accessed by boat or car. With dozens of walks in this book ranging from less than 1 mile and up to 8 miles exploring riverbank, reedbed, woodland, marsh and even beach dunes proves there is so much more to see than you may first realise.

Acle

River Bure

Acle

Acle is a large village with a history dating back nearly two thousand years to Roman times when a small port was located here. There are several shops and pubs dotted around the village with free parking available by the library and moorings around Acle Bridge. Other than Stokesby, Acle is the last settlement before the long stretch of the River Bure to Great Yarmouth. The surrounding countryside is largely grazing marsh and agricultural land with a number of walks that takes in the beauty of the area. Acle also has excellent public transport links with regular bus and train services to Great Yarmouth and Norwich from the village centre. Included on the map is the permissive footpath that links Acle Bridge to the main village to avoid walking along the main road.

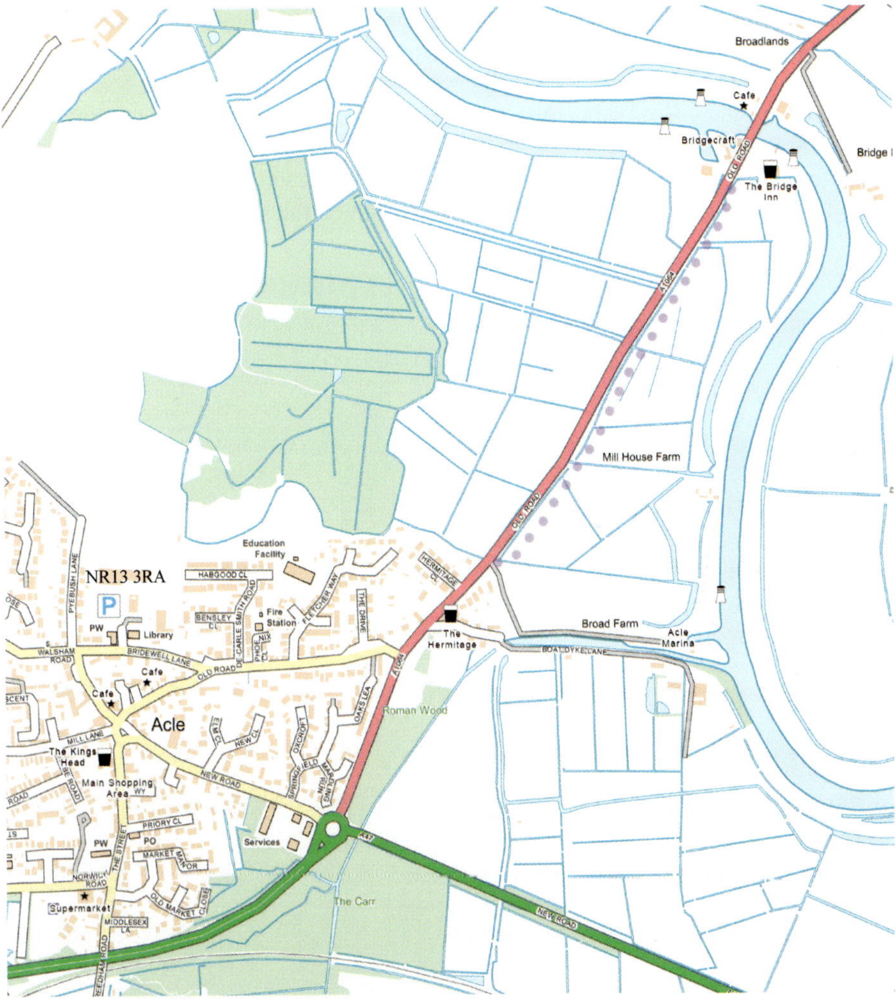

Walk 1:
St Edmund's Church

Distance: 6.0km (3.73 Miles)
Time: 2 Hours
Parking: Roadside Layby **NR13 3AT**

From Acle Bridge, follow the public footpath pointed towards the Bridge Inn (marked as the Weavers Way) and continue along the top of the flood bank south, keeping the river on the left. The path passes the base of an old mill by some moorings and continues to head south to Acle Marina where it swings to the right along the dyke and up to the minor road of Boat Dyke Lane. At the road you need to turn left briefly to a footpath straight ahead along a water filled ditch to the south. This path continues in a relatively straight line to cross the A47 and along the path opposite over the railway. Continue south until a track intercepts from the left where you need to turn right along Damgate Lane. Follow the lane to junction and turn right along Reedham Road, under the A47 overpass and up to St Edmund's Church in the centre of Acle. After exploring the church continue north along the main high street, past numerous shops and take aways to the Kings Head where the road splits. Follow the road straight ahead to the right (Old Road) past the Olive Tree cafe and to the east up to the main road. Bear left along the main road past The Hermitage to the edge of the village. Cross the road to the track on the opposite side to the permissive footpath on the left running parallel to the main road back to Acle Bridge.

St Edmund's Church, Acle

St Edmund's Church & St Mary's Priory

The beautiful Grade I listed church of St Edmund in Acle is one of only 124 round tower churches in Norfolk. Most of the church dates to the 13th and 14th Centuries with the possibility of the tower being older and dating to the 12th Century. Records also show that there was a Priory somewhere in the area, with old maps indicating the main site being near the present day church and a Priory Cell located out into the marshes by Acle Bridge Inn. Although nothing remains above ground, earthworks are recorded in the fields behind The Bridge Inn which potentially show a precinct wall of an Augustinian house founded before 1272. Medieval pottery and numerous inhumation burials have been found in the area adding to the likelihood of this being the original site of the Priory.

The Bridge Inn, Acle

Walk 2:
Upton & The River Bure

Distance: 6.5km (4.04 Miles)
Time: 2 Hours
Parking: Roadside Layby **NR13 3AT**

From Acle Bridge, keep the Bridge Inn on the left and follow the main road briefly to the permissive path that runs parallel to the road and up to the edge of Acle. Once at the village follow the road briefly again and turn right along Old Road. Bear right down Bridewell Lane at the fork and shortly after the Methodist Church turn right down Pyebush Lane. At the end is a cemetery where the path bears left along its edge and then along a field boundary to the isolated St Mary's Church in Fishley and a farm track. Continue across the field opposite up to a small wood where the path passes through and turns right up to the road in Upton. Turn right along the road and follow this gently round to the right and at the fork, keep left. The lane turns into a track and follows a couple of gentle bends up to a gate with footpaths on the left and right. Turn right and follow the path through the woods. At the other side the path turns right and then left to the next wood and along the left edge of this up to the River Bure. Turn right along the path behind the riverside properties and then up onto the riverbank on the left. Follow this back to Acle Bridge, taking care through the boatyard and back to the start.

St Mary's Church. Fishley

Four Windmills seen from Acle Bridge

St Mary's Church. Fishley

The isolated church of St Mary in Fishley, complete with its Norman round tower is a lovely Grade II* building, and the opportunity to have a look around should not be missed. Dating back to the 12th Century the church was largely restored in 1861, however the tower was virtually untouched making this a fine example.

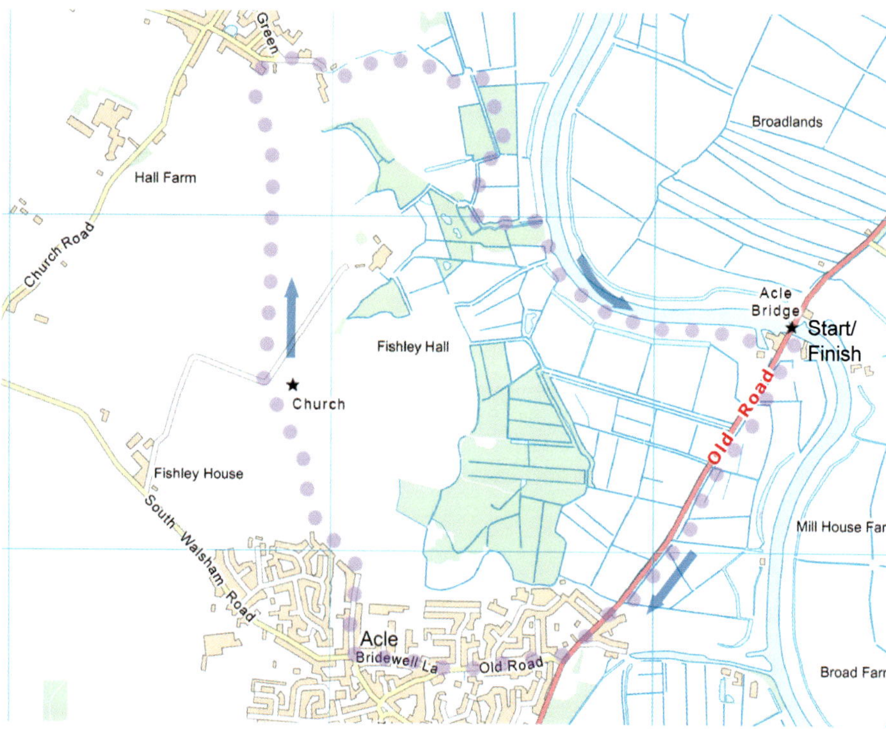

Barton Turf

River Ant

Barton Turf

Barton Turf is a small village on the far northern edge of Barton Broad. It has a large boatyard with free moorings close by and a car park at the staithe. The village no longer has any pubs or shops, with the nearest being at Neatishead (The White Horse & Small Convenience Store). The village is surrounded by open countryside making it the perfect place to take a short walk away from the busy waterways, especially to the lovely parish church roughly a mile from the staithe. Cox's Boatyard is the main boatyard in the village providing private moorings, boat repairs, servicing and restoration.

Barton Turf Staithe

Barton Broad

Barton Broad is the second largest broad in Norfolk and under the management of the Norfolk Wildlife Trust. It covers an area of 410 acres with access available on the southern side at Irstead or from the north at Sutton. Boaters should take care travelling across the broad and remain within the guideposts to avoid grounding in the shallow waters.

Barton Broad

Walk 3:
St Michael's Church

Distance: 3.9km (2.4 Miles)
Time: 1 Hour 15 Minutes
Parking: Staithe Car Park **NR12 8AZ**

From Barton Turf Staithe follow Staithe Road to the west into the village centre. Continue up to the junction with Hall Road by the village sign and turn left. Take the second right along Church Road and follow the lane up to St Michael and All Angels Church. Just past the church is a public footpath on the right across the open field, follow this through two fields and up to the road at a small wood. Turn right along the lane and follow this up to the junction and turn left. Just ahead bear right at the village sign along Staithe Road and back to the car park and moorings.

St Michael's Church

The remote Church of St Michael sits around a mile from the village centre and dates back to the 14th Century with the tower being built in the 15th Century. Inside the church is a fantastically preserved medieval painted rood screen which is a must see for visitors to the church.

St Michael's Church, Barton Turf

Walk 4: Pennygate

Distance: 3.5km (2.2 Miles)
Time: 1 Hour
Parking: Staithe Car Park **NR12 8AZ**

Beginning at Barton Staithe head west along Staithe Road into the village of Barton Turf and up to the junction by the village sign. Turn left and take the first lane on the right (School Lane) and continue for about 500m to a public footpath on the right across the open field. Take this path into the tiny village of Pennygate. At the road turn left and immediately right along Berry Hall Road as it completes a wide curve around agricultural land and towards Barton Turf. At the fork bear left and at the next fork bear left again along Common Road up to Staithe Road and turn left back to the car park and moorings.

Fields around Barton Turf

Belaugh

River Bure

Belaugh

Belaugh (pronounced bee-la) is a tiny village along the River Bure between Coltishall and Hoveton offering a small area of free parking and mooring at the staithe. With no shops or pubs, it offers little to visitors except a beautiful rural feel and tranquil waters to relax by. The nearby church is worth the short walk to with its own moorings along a narrow path which is a rarity on the Broads. The village has very few public footpaths making circular walks difficult but a short stroll close by the river to Coltishall Common is worth it as well as following the lanes around the village. The nearest shops and pubs are in either Hoveton or Coltishall approximately 2 miles away by road.

Walk 5:
St Peter's Church

Distance: 0.7km (0.4 Miles)
Time: 20 Minutes
Parking: Staithe Car Park **NR12 8XA**

From the small parking area and Staithe in Belaugh head south along the road, keeping the river over to the right, up to the parish church. Continue into the church yard over to the right hand side where a narrow path leads down to a private staithe for the church and some lovely views over the river. Backtrack to the road by the church and turn right, then at the junction ahead turn left. After about 80m there is a footpath on the left leading between properties up to the road and then turn right back to the staithe.

Belaugh Staithe

St Peter's Church, Belaugh

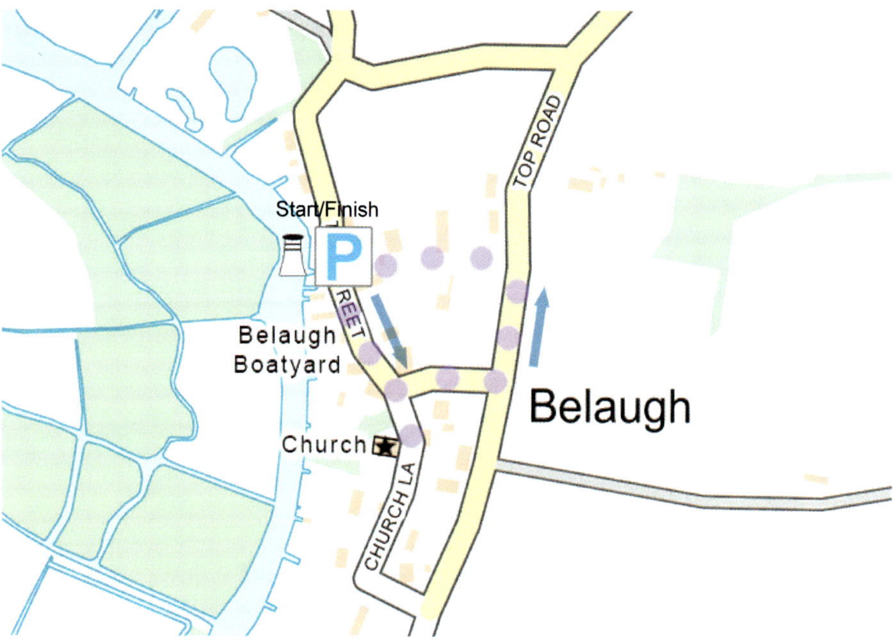

St Peter's Church, Belaugh

The lovely church of St Peter sits on a hill about 10m above the surrounding marsh and river. The church dates to the 12th Century, with the tower being built in the 15th Century and given the protection of a Grade 1 listing. The church has its own private moorings down a footpath alongside the church yard which is exceptionally rare on the Broads and the perfect place to sit and enjoy the views of the River Bure.

Church Staithe

Coltishall

River Bure

Coltishall

At the end of the River Bure navigation is the lovely village of Coltishall, with its large staithe, numerous pubs and interesting history. The Rising Sun and Kings Head overlook the pastures and gently flowing waters by the staithe, with a third, the Red Lion, just in the village centre. On the north side of the village is one of the stations for the Bure Valley Railway, a narrow gauge train linking nearby Wroxham to Aylsham. The post office and store sits just behind the Kings Head with a larger convenience store and multiple takeaways in the village centre. Alongside the takeaways is the local pharmacy, butchers and just across the river s a lovely farm shop, deli and The Recruiting Sergeant pub.

St John the Baptist, Coltishall

The stunning Grade I listed church of St John the Baptist dates back to the 15th Century and largely rebuilt in 1865. Some elements of the church date from before this indicating the possibility of an earlier church on the site in the 13th Century.

Coltishall Staithe

St Theobald's Church, Great Hautbois

The stunning ruins of St Theobald's Church lies close to the River Bure and date back almost 1000 years to the 11th Century making it one of the oldest churches in the area. There's even a chance the Nave may be Late Saxon, with a slightly later Saxo-Norman round tower. The ruins are protected as a Grade II* listed building.

Walk 6:
Horstead Mill

Distance: 3.0km (1.9 Miles)
Time: 1 Hour 15 Minutes
Parking: Staithe Car Park **NR12 7EA**

From the staithe at Coltishall, head onto the road and turn left. Follow the road for 950m to the west, past the post office and church to the road junction just by Coltishall Island (the petrol station). Turn left to follow the road over the River Bure and immediately on the left, take the footpath along the riverbank to the south. Follow this riverside path for about 400m to which point you will arrive at the remains of Horstead Mill. Head across the bridge alongside the mill to the other side and turn left. Follow the path round to Coltishall Lock and cross the river here. Turn left and follow the permissive footpath north along the river. After about 300m cross the bridge on the right, follow the field edge on the left and cross a second bridge. Head up to the road and turn right, then follow the road for about 900m to the east to get back to Coltishall Common.

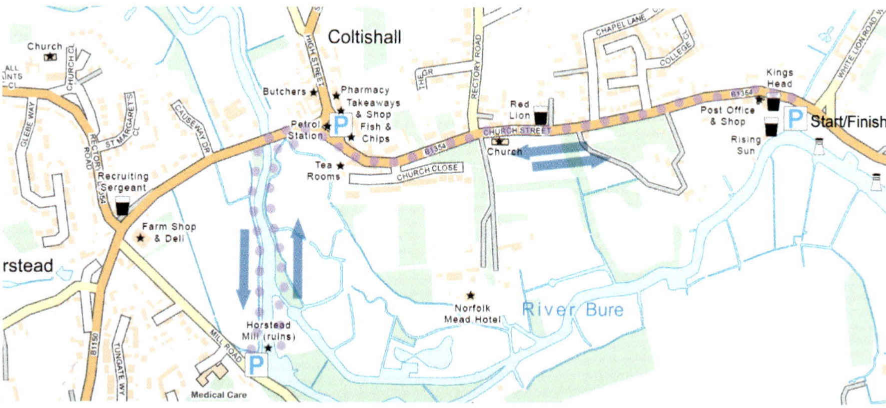

River Bure at Horstead Mill

Horstead Mill

Walk 7: Little Hautbois Hall	**Distance:** 8.7km (5.4 Miles) **Time:** 3 Hours **Parking:** Staithe Car Park **NR12 7EA**

From Coltishall Staithe head out onto the road and turn left. Follow the road past the parish church and then round a gentle bend up to a junction by a fuel station. Turn left towards the bridge and after just a few metres is a footpath on the right along the eastern side of the River Bure. This section of the river is not navigable to motor cruisers so it is very quiet and full of wildlife. Stick to the riverbank path until you reach the road but along here you may notice the ruins of St Theobald's Church on the right which is close to the site of Hautbois Castle.

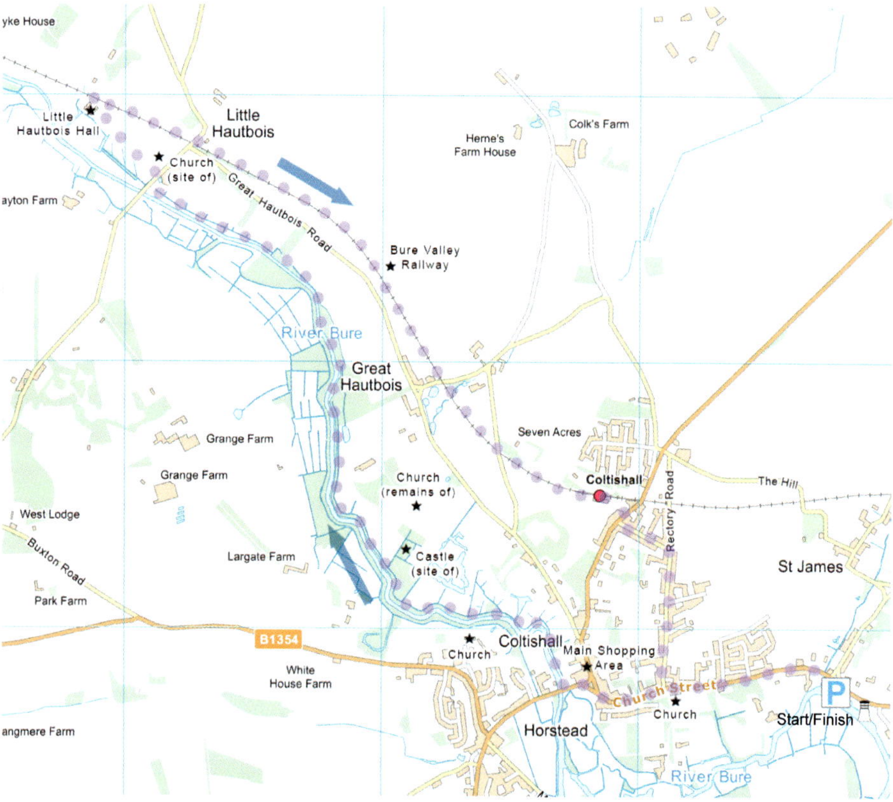

Great Hautbois Castle

The site of Hautbois Castle is just over 100m from the ruins of St Theobald's Church and very close to the line of the present River Bure. The castle was built in 1312 with the foundations of a porter's lodge and house remaining in fairly good condition. A raised platform just to the east may have been a bailey containing more buildings associated with the castle.

Little Hautbois

The approach to Little Hautbois Hall hides some interesting history. The field on the right was the location of St Mary's Church and Hospital which was founded in the 13th Century. Throughout the centuries parts of the structure were demolished and by 1535 only a chapel remained which in turn was abandoned by the late 16th Century when the nearby village also became deserted.

Once at the road turn right and then take the driveway to Hautbois Hall on the left. Follow the driveway towards the hall (on the right here was the site of St Mary's Church) and once there head round the side of the property to the railway line. This is the Bure Valley Railway and has a footpath alongside. Turn right and follow this path until you reach Coltishall Station. Follow the track out onto the road and turn right and shortly ahead turn left down Westbourne Road. At the end of the lane turn right and follow Rectory Road to the end where you will encounter the Church of St John the Baptist. Turn left and follow the road back to Coltishall Staithe.

Little Hautbois Hall

Little Hautbois Hall (pronounced 'Hobbis') is a rare and stunning Elizabethan house made of brick and dating to the late 16th Century. The Grade II* listed building has been painstakingly restored over the last few years retaining many original features.

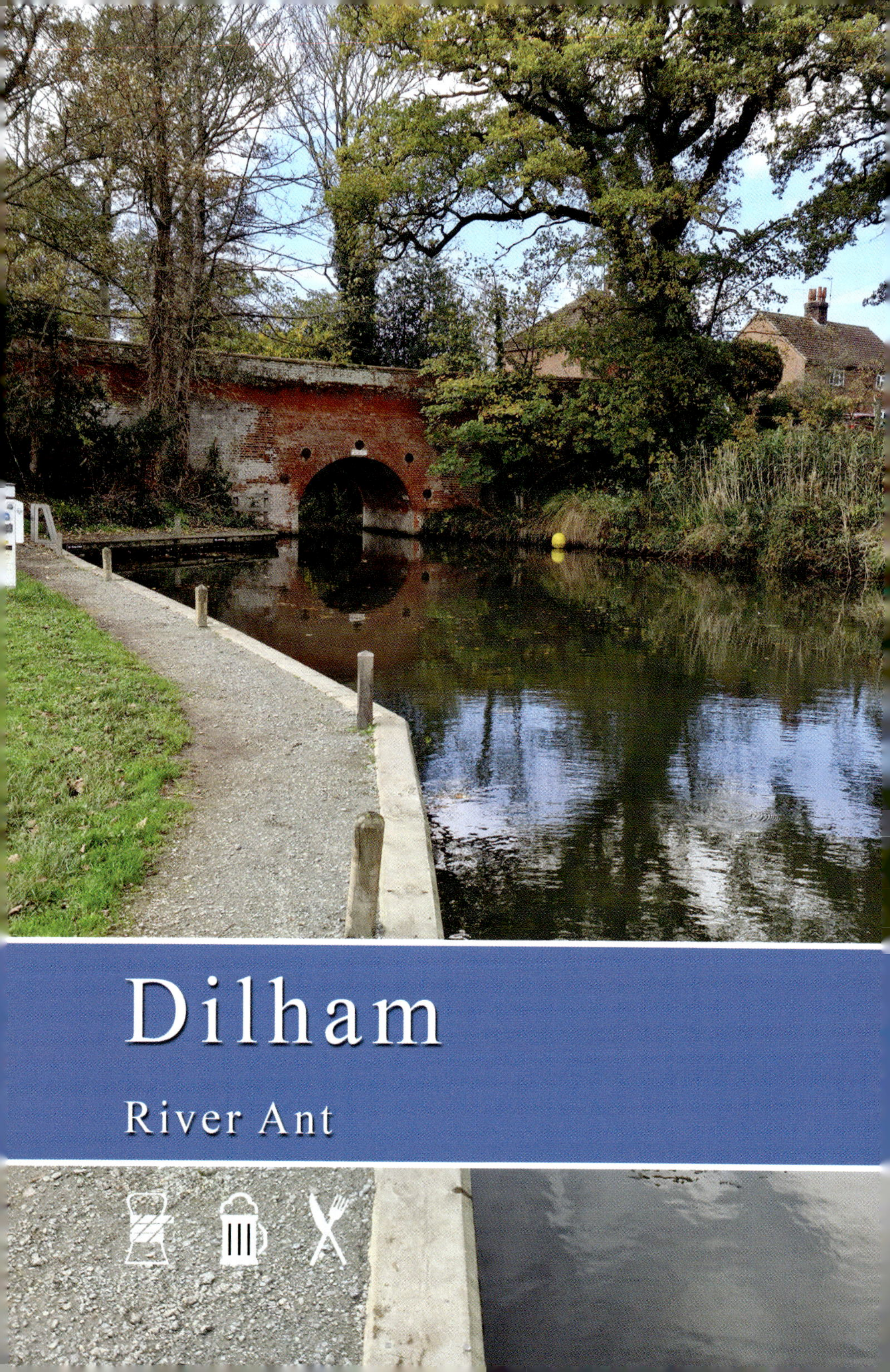

Dilham

River Ant

Dilham

Dilham is a small village on the northern edge of the Broads close to the town of Stalham. There is a small staithe offering free moorings and a tiny area to park up along the road just a short walk from the Cross Keys Inn. There are no other facilities in the village with the closest shops being at Stalham several miles away and another pub, The Smallburgh Crown just a mile or so down the road. Surrounding Dilham is some beautiful broadland countryside including the newly restored North Walsham & Dilham Canal which is a sanctuary for wildlife.

Walk 8:
Dilham Church

Distance: 3.1km (1.9 Miles)
Time: 1 Hour 15 Minutes
Parking: Layby at Staithe **NR28 9PS**

From Dilham Staithe, head onto the road and turn left leading you south into the village centre. Pass the Cross Keys Inn, bearing right along The Street and eventually up to the A149 Main Road. Turn right along the pavement and just ahead there is a country lane on the opposite side of the road. A public footpath just to the right of this country lane leads you parallel to the main road heading north west and eventually emerges at the main road again. Cross carefully onto the bridleway opposite and follow it away from the main road for about ½ a mile along the field edge to emerge on a road by Dilham Church. Turn right and follow the lane east up to the junction (it's along this stretch you may see the tower of Dilham Hall). At the road junction turn right and follow it back to Dilham Staithe.

Dilham Castle

Dilham may be a small quiet village now but centuries ago a fortified manor house was located on the site of Dilham Hall. A single tower remains of what was Dilham Castle and probably formed part of the gatehouse for this defensive structure. It is believed to date to the 15th Century and was restored in 1904 and now protected as a Grade II listed building and scheduled ancient monument.

Dilham Tower

Walk 9:
Dilham Canal

Distance: 6.2km (3.9 Miles)
Time: 2 Hours
Parking: Layby at Staithe **NR28 9PS**

From Dilham Staithe, head onto the road and turn right, taking the first lane on the right almost straight away. At the junction turn right following Broad Fen Lane south and gently round to the left. Once at the end of the road the lane turns into a track and continues along the tree line and woods. Keep right along the straight path with the woods on the right and follow the track as it turns north towards Tonnage Bridge and a property. The path turns right past the property and up to Tonnage Bridge where there is a footpath on the left along the western side of the Canal. Follow the path north, keeping the canal on the right, and at no point turn away from the water. It's just over 2.1km of riverbank walking with several footbridges until there is a split in the path close to Honing Lock just before woodland. Keep along the riverbank path over the footbridge and through the woods to arrive at Honing Lock and its lovely small waterfall. Do not cross the lock, instead backtrack to the split just as you leave the wood and turn right leading across the open field to a gate and along a track to a house. Follow the path round the left side of the house and up to the road. Turn left and follow the road south for about ¾ of a mile to Dilham Staithe.

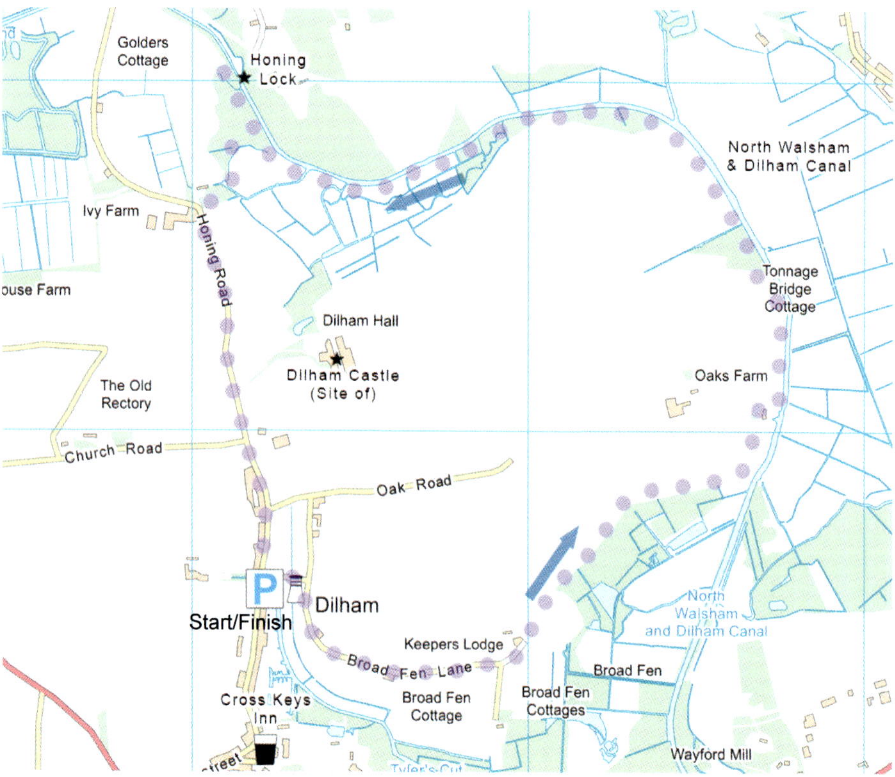

Honing Lock

North Walsham and Dilham Canal

The North Walsham & Dilham Canal is unique in Norfolk, being the only wherry sailing canal with locks. Opening in 1826, the canal is 9 miles long and once transported goods from around North Walsham towards the coast. In recent years the canal has undergone a massive restoration scheme and now offers boat trips up and down the waterways.

Dilham Canal

Great Yarmouth

River Yare & River Bure

Great Yarmouth

Great Yarmouth is the main coastal town in the Broads and a hive of activity during the peak holiday season. During July and August it can be difficult to find a mooring or parking space so arriving early is key. The yacht station offers boaters basic facilities and is located about a 10 minute walk from the train station and about 15 minutes from the town centre. The seafront offers plenty of amusements including several piers, arcades, the Sea-Life Centre, Pleasure Beach and much more. Public transport links are excellent, with regular bus services to surrounding villages as well as a route across the Broads to Norwich via Acle. The railway station provides regular services to Acle, Lingwood, Brundall and Norwich throughout the day. Breydon Water sits to the west of Great Yarmouth and is a large expanse of open water with a narrow navigable channel marked by large posts. Seek advice from the yacht station prior to crossing due to risk of grounding. This large estuary is also a nature reserve managed by the RSPB and has one hide that overlooks vast expanses of mudflat and salt marsh. The town also has some of the best preserved medieval town walls in England including numerous surviving defensive towers.

Medieval Town Walls

Great Yarmouth has some of the best preserved and complete Medieval Town Walls in England and dates to 28th September 1261 when King Henry III granted permission to fortify. A superb historic walk along the town walls is included in this chapter.

Great Yarmouth Yacht Station

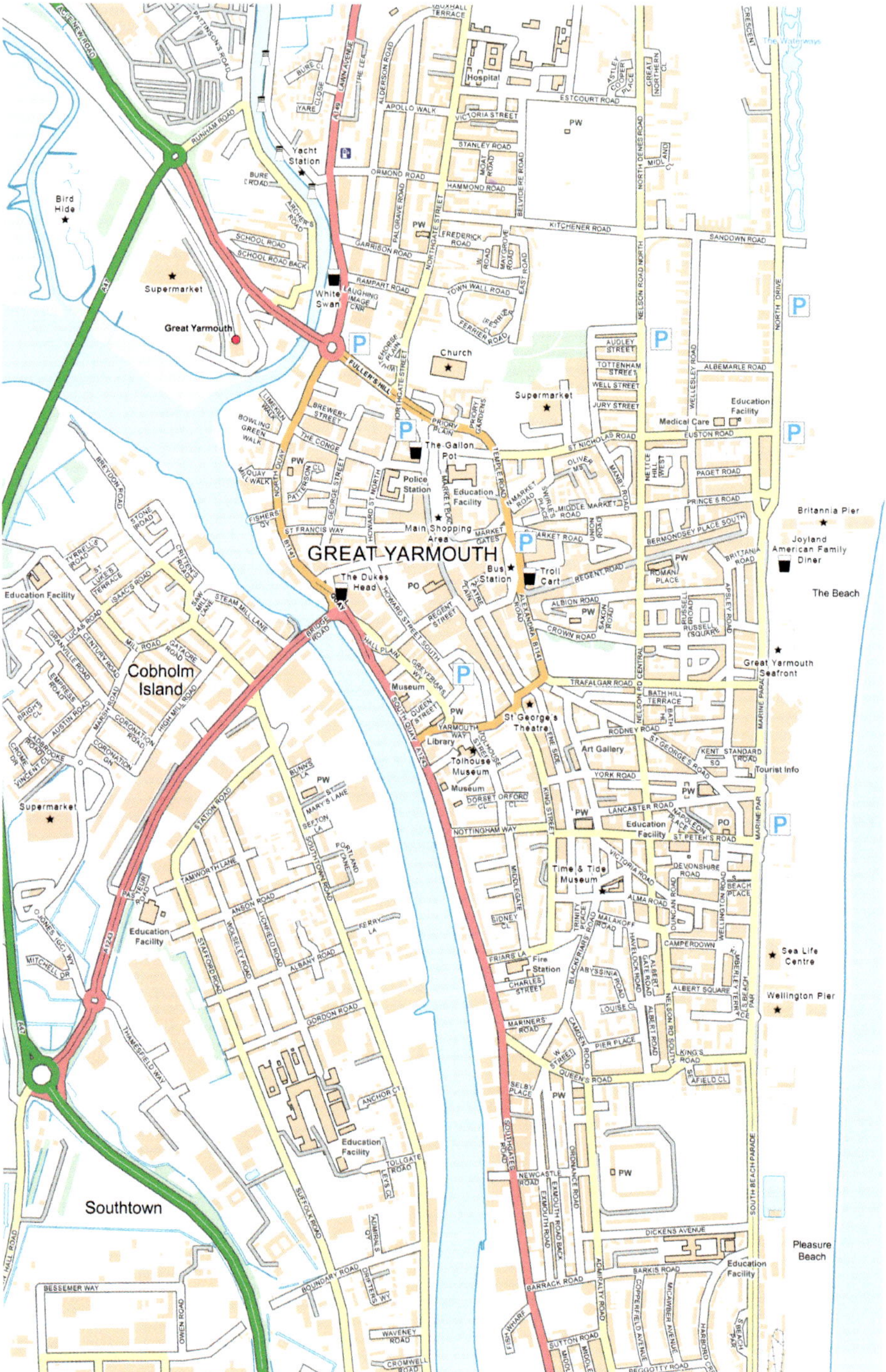
GREAT YARMOUTH
Cobholm Island
Southtown
Bird Hide
Supermarket
Great Yarmouth
Yacht Station
White Swan
Laughing Image Cnr
Church
The Gallon Pot
Police Station
Education Facility
Main Shopping Area
Bus Station
Troll Cart
The Dukes Head
PO
Museum
PW
Library
Tolhouse Museum
St George's Theatre
Art Gallery
Time & Tide Museum
Fire Station
Hospital
Medical Care
Britannia Pier
Joyland American Family Diner
The Beach
Great Yarmouth Seafront
Tourist Info
Sea Life Centre
Wellington Pier
Pleasure Beach
The Waterways
Runham Road
Acle New Road
A47
A149
A1243
B1141
Lawn Avenue
Bure Road
Archer's Road
School Road
School Road Back
Rampart Road
Garrison Road
Ormond Road
Apollo Walk
Alderson Road
Palgrave Road
Northgate Street
Victoria Street
Stanley Road
Hammond Road
Frederick Road
Belvidere Road
Estcourt Road
Kitchener Road
Sandown Road
North Denes Road
Nelson Road North
Wellesley Road
North Drive
Town Wall Road
Ferrier Road
Fuller's Hill
Brewery Street
The Conge
Priory Plain
Priory Gardens
Temple Road
North Quay
George Street
Howard St North
St Francis Way
Market Place
Market Gates
Regent Road
Regent Street
Howard Street South
Hall Plain
Greyfriars Wy
South Quay
Queen Street
Yarmouth Way
Tolhouse Street
Alexandra Road
Albion Road
Crown Road
Trafalgar Road
Nelson Rd Central
Rodney Road
St George's Road
King Street
York Road
Lancaster Road
St Peter's Road
Nottingham Way
Middlegate
Victoria Road
Alma Road
Devonshire Road
Duncan Road
Wellington Road
Camperdown
Albert Square
Nelson Rd South
Kimberley Terrace
Marine Parade
South Beach Parade
Friars' La
Charles Street
Blackfriars' Road
Abyssinia Road
Havelock Road
Mariners' Road
Pier Place
King's Road
Queen's Road
Southgates Road
Newcastle Road
Exmouth Road
Ordnance Road
Admiralty Road
Dickens Avenue
Barkis Road
Copperfield Avenue
Micawber Avenue
Barrack Road
Sutton Road
Peggotty Road
Fish Wharf
Bridge Road
Steam Mill Lane
Mill Road
Century Road
Granville Road
Lucas Road
Marsh Road
High Mill Road
Coronation Road
Austin Road
Breydon Road
Station Road
Tamworth Lane
Anson Road
Wolseley Road
Lichfield Road
Stafford Road
Albany Road
Gordon Road
Southtown Road
Suffolk Road
Boundary Road
Thamesfield Way
Pasteur Road
Mitchell Dr
Bessemer Way
Owen Road
Tollgate Road
Anchor Ct
Waveney Road
Cromwell Road

Nelson's Monument

Set back from the seafront and away from the crowds is Nelson's Monument, also known as the Britannia Monument or Norfolk Pillar and stands to a height of 133ft. Built between 1817 - 1819, it was the first monument in England to Admiral Lord Nelson and protected with a Grade I listing.

Walk 10:
RSPB Breydon Water

Distance: 2.6km (1.6 Miles)
Time: 1 Hour 30 Minutes
Parking: Fullers Hill Car Park **NR30 1BF**

From the yacht station follow the riverbank south towards the road bridge. Turn right over the bridge and up to the traffic lights 150m ahead. Cross over the road and follow the path towards the Train Station. Behind the station is a supermarket and to the left is the estuary wall. Head up to the wall which borders the estuary and follow it past the car park and under Breydon Bridge. Beyond you will see the bird hide. You can extend the walk by continuing along Breydon Water before turning back and retracing your steps back to the Yacht Station. Car Parking is available at Fullers Hill close to the Yacht Station.

Breydon Water Bird Hide

Thousands of Birds on Breydon Water

Walk 11:
Medieval Town Walls

Distance: 4.0km (2.5 Miles)
Time: 2 Hours
Parking: Fullers Hill Car Park **NR30 1BF**

From Great Yarmouth Yacht Station head to the end of the moorings and over the flood defence wall to the main road. Turn right and follow the pavement up to the first Medieval Tower seen on the walk. Cross the road carefully and follow Rampart Road opposite which was the line of the old town wall. At the junction at the end of the road continue opposite down Town Wall Road where the wall resumes to a corner tower. Turn right down Ferrier Road with the town wall to the right and up to the unique octagonal tower.

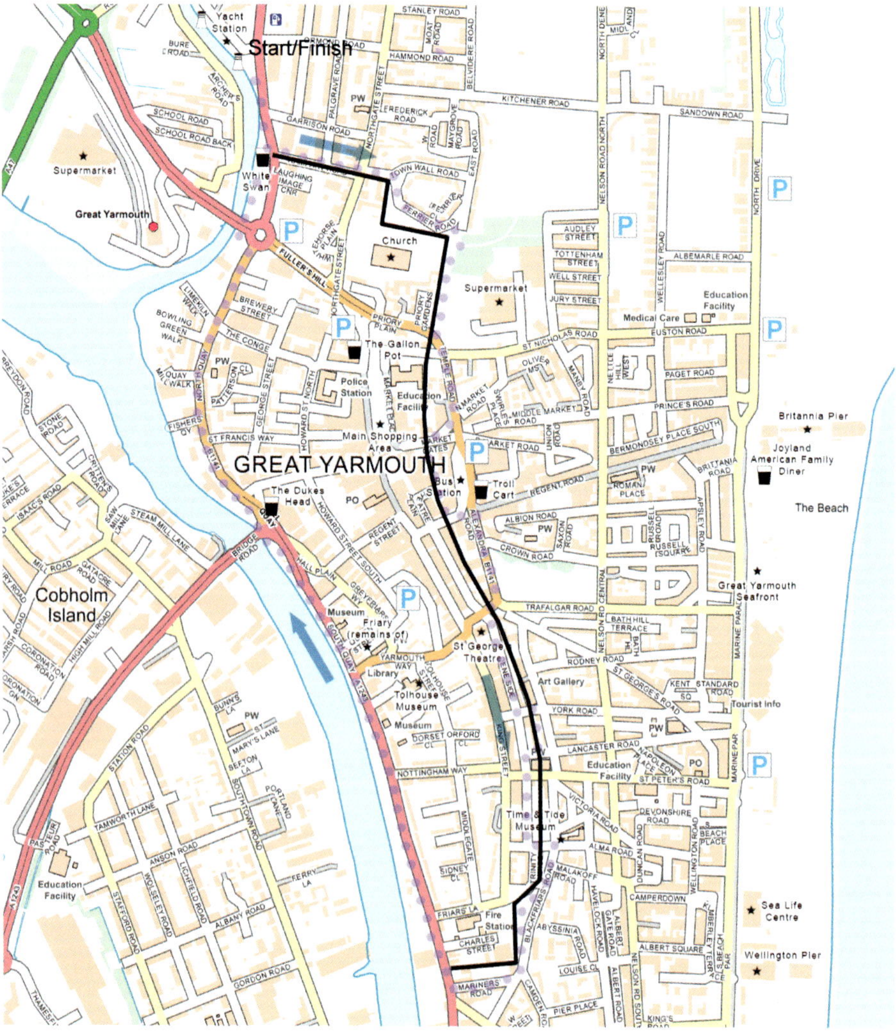

North West Tower

Just beyond this tower is a gate and entry into the church yard. Head into the churchyard and turn right then left straight away to follow the path south towards the Supermarket Car Park and up to a path along the town wall. At the road turn left and use the crossing just ahead to cross to the right hand side of the road and turn left along Temple Road towards the large shopping centre of Market Gates just ahead. Half way down this section there is another tower tucked in the buildings on the right. Once at Market Gates turn right towards the historic market area and after just a short way there is a path on the left directly alongside the old town wall. Keep on the right hand side by the continuous arches and stick to it past another tower and to the road. Follow the road in the same direction to arrive by the main entrance to Market Gates. Turn left to the bus station and then turn right along Alexandra Road heading south with St George's Park just over to the left. Continue to the end of the park (halfway along here is another tower just over to the right) and at the junction turn right towards St George's Theatre. Opposite the theatre was the site of Great Yarmouth Castle, probably 12th Century and demolished in 1621.

Town Walls

Turn left just before the theatre down Dene Side and then turn left down York Road. After just a few metres turn right down the alleyway which marks the line of the town wall and once at the end you will be at St Spyridon Church. Turn right and then left up to the junction and then continue straight ahead down Dene Side which runs along the side of the medieval town wall. At the junction turn left through a break in the town wall with the Time and Tide Museum just ahead. At the junction turn right and follow Blackfriars Road towards the next tower and continue to just after is a small green backed by the town wall close to its full height. Follow the wall to the next tower which is one of the most impressive and then round to the right along Mariners' Road. At the end of the road turn right along South Quay past the industrial works and onto the historic quay, passing the Nelson Museum and National Trusts Elizabethan House Museum and up to Great Yarmouth Town Hall. Two very worthwhile detours to see the ruined friary and Tolhouse Museum are highly recommended here before continuing past the town hall. Follow the quay ahead past Haven Bridge and then along North Quay as the road gently bends round to the right past a tall tower block and more industrial workings until you arrive at the large roundabout. Bear left down to the river and head under the bridge to the north side which leads back to the Yacht Station.

Time and Tide Museum

The Time and Tide is a museum set within one of the countries best preserved Victorian Herring curing works and explores the history of Great Yarmouth through the years. There are various exhibitions including a reconstruction of a typical 'Row' from 1913, films and other displays.

Blackfriars

In the peak of Medieval Great Yarmouth there were as many as five religious houses, all of which have been destroyed except Blackfriars. This Franciscan Friary was founded in 1226 and extended on several occasions throughout its first 100 years. The remains are protected as a Grade I listed building and scheduled ancient monument.

Tolhouse Museum

The Grade I listed Tolhouse, now a museum, is a fortified merchants house dating to 1150. Throughout the centuries the building has been repurposed, being used as a prison between 1261 - 1875, a Town Hall, Police Station, Courthouse and Toll Office.

The Golden Mile

The mile long seafront of Great Yarmouth, better known as the Golden Mile attracts millions of visitors each year, with dozens of shops, restaurants, takeaways, amusements and indoor and outdoor attractions including Joyland, the Pleasure Beach and Sea-life Centre. There are two piers, the Britannia Pier and Wellington Pier about a kilometre from each other with numerous attractions sandwiched in between.

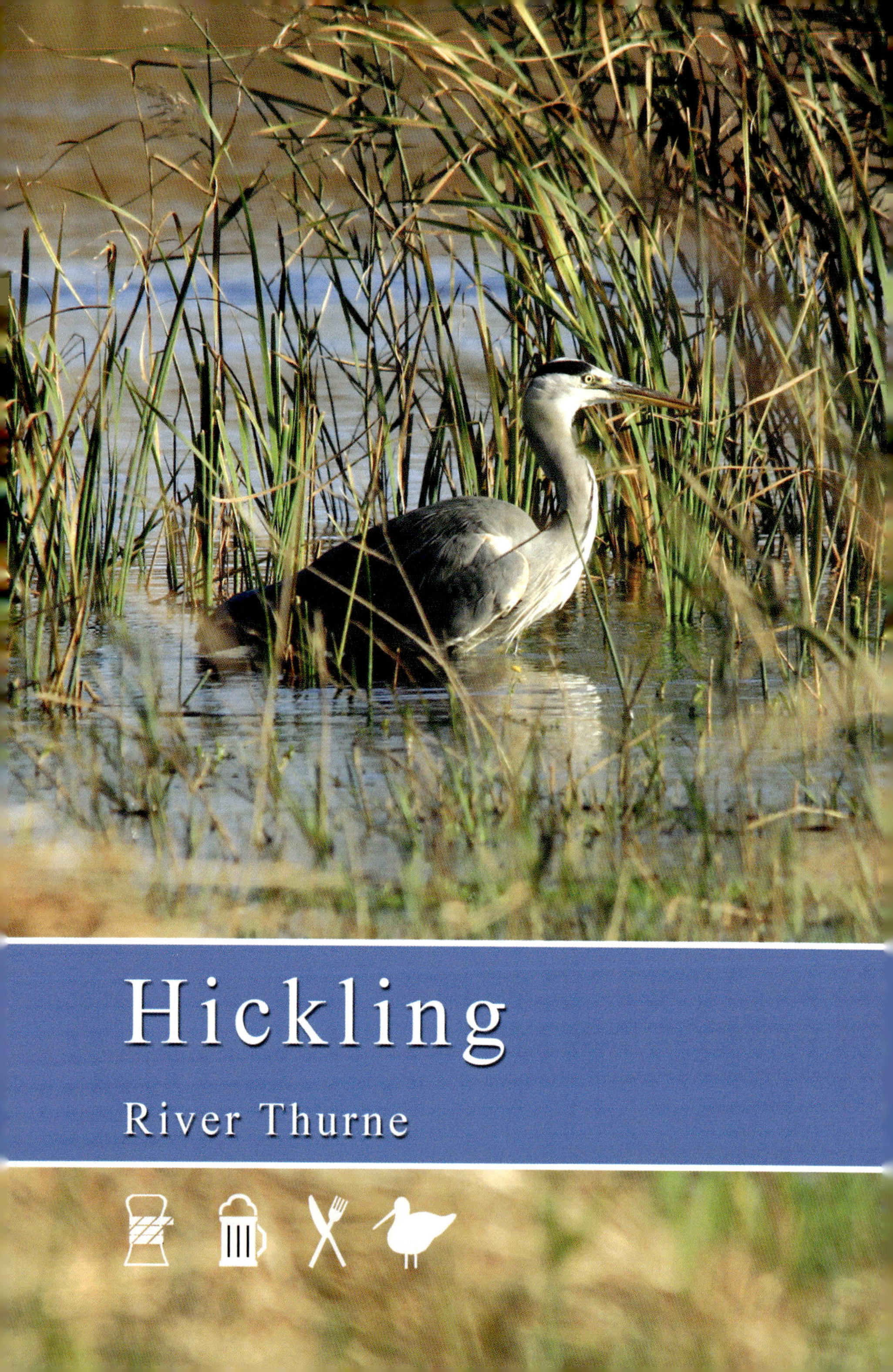

Hickling

River Thurne

Hickling

Hickling is a small village on the northern tip of the largest Broad in Norfolk; Hickling Broad. The staithe offers moorings and a small area for parking by the Pleasure Boat Inn with another pub; the Greyhound Inn located just ¼ of a mile up the road in the village centre. Just over a mile out of the village to the east is the Norfolk Wildlife Trust Hickling Broad Nature Reserve, one of the most wildlife rich areas on the Broads and home to rare species such as Bittern, Bearded Tit and the only place in the county you can see the Common Crane. Set back from the main village is the parish church of St Mary with the site of an Augustinian Priory founded in 1185 situated just slightly to the north but sadly on private ground. Hickling Broad itself has the largest surface area of any Broad and one of the largest expanses of water in East Anglia. Most of the broad is very shallow, with the navigation channel through the centre being only 1.5m deep.

Norfolk Wildlife Trust Hickling Broad

Norfolk Wildlife Trust Hickling Broad Reserve is one of the best nature reserves on the Broads. It has a mixture of habitats, ranging from open water, woodland and meadow to acres of reedbed. This mosaic attracts such a diverse range of wildlife including some of the rarest species in the country like the Bittern, Marsh Harrier and Crane. The two hides overlooking Swim Coots and Rush Hill and the Viewing Tower are only accessible via a boat trip from the Nature Reserve which are booked in the visitor centre.

Hickling Broad Nature Reserve

Walk 12:
Hickling Green

Distance: 2.6km (1.6 Miles)
Time: 1 Hour
Parking: Staithe Car Park **NR12 0YW**

From the moorings follow the trackway that leads to the road alongside the Staithe. Turn right and follow the country lane past Whispering Reeds boatyard. Along this stretch of road there are some nice views over the fields to the nearby mill on the left. Continue to follow this country lane past beautiful flint cottages to The Greyhound Inn. Turn left at the road junction and continue past the car park and chapel, up to the last house on the right. There is a footpath on the edge of the field on the right here so you do not have to walk on the road. On arrival at the crossroads turn left which is signposted to Hickling Broad. This small country lane takes you back to the moorings and car park.

Hickling Green Mill

The large 8 storey mill on the left along this section was built in 1817 and stands 71ft high with a traditional white boat shaped cap. The mill has been given a Grade II* listing.

Walk 13: Hickling Church

Distance: 4.4km (2.7 Miles)
Time: 1 Hour 30 Minutes
Parking: Staithe Car Park NR12 0YW

From the staithe follow the road to the right and after 600m turn right along Stubb Road. After 200m turn left along The Causeway and follow it to the junction, turn right and then left along a footpath which leads in a straight line along the edge of the field to the church. Once at the church turn left along the road to the junction and turn left again. The path passes through an area of Hickling known as Town Street, with a sharp bend right followed by a sharp bend left and into Hickling Green. Turn left down Stubb Road past the Greyhound Pub and follow the lane back to the staithe.

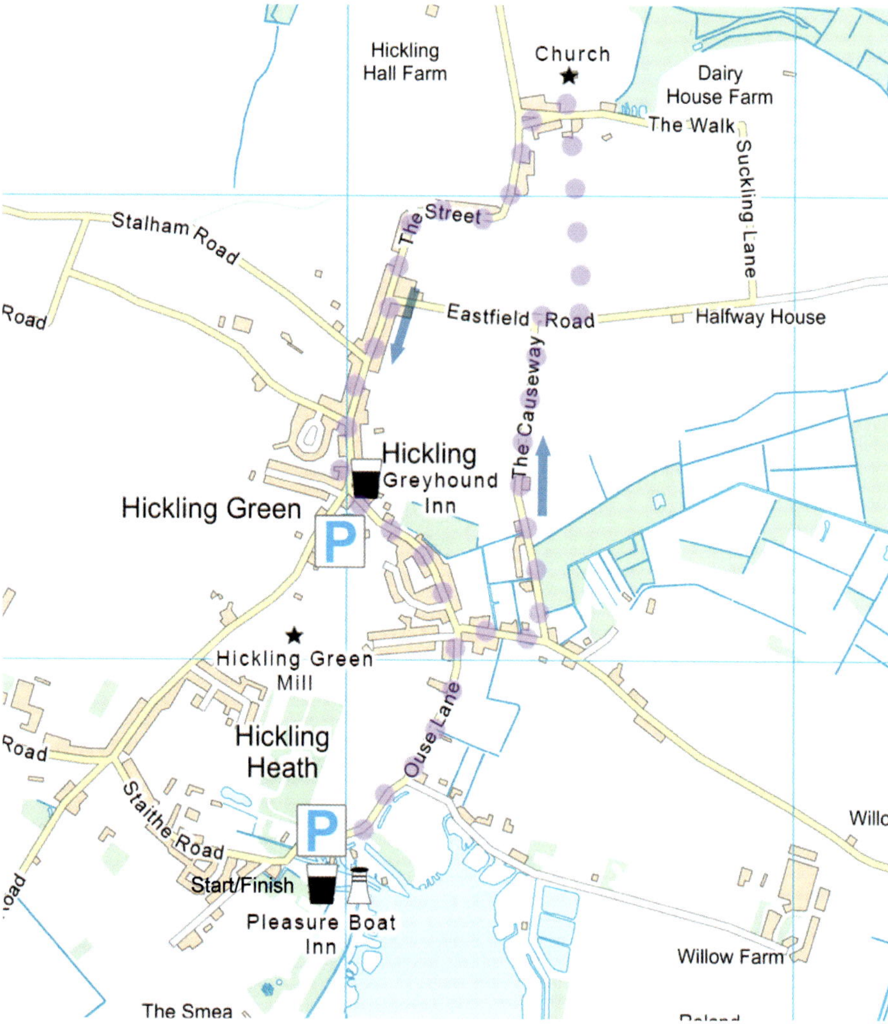

Hickling Broad

St Mary's Church, Hickling

The Church of St Mary in Hickling was built in the late 14th Century with significant restorations in the late 19th Century. The church has been given the protection of a Grade II* listing.

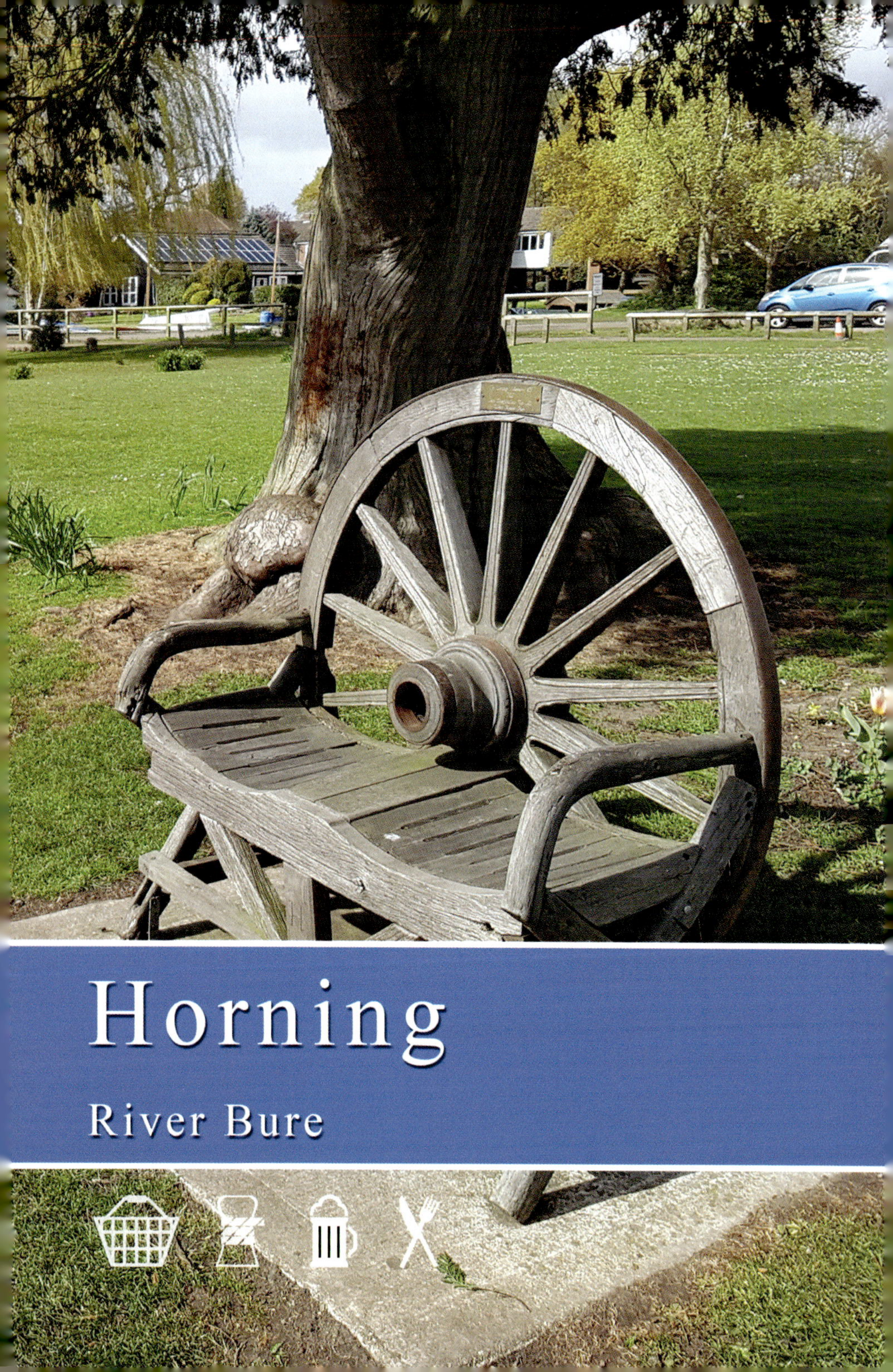

Horning

River Bure

Horning

Horning sits high on the itinerary list for most visitors to the Norfolk Broads thanks to its charming location and enough amenities to accommodate most tastes including a takeaway, cafes and restaurants. It has built up along a straight section of the River Bure starting at the Ferry Inn on its south side and continuing north west almost three quarters of a mile to the Swan Inn. The staithe overlooks a busy stretch of river being the only way to Wroxham by boat and has regular launches of the Southern Comfort offering river trips to Ranworth. One of the main attractions in Horning is the children's woodland adventure park known as BeWilderwood located about half a mile from the staithe. On the outskirts of the village is the site of RAF Neatishead which is also the location of the Radar Museum which is open from April to October and run by volunteers and only a 20 minute walk from the staithe. There are areas of 24 hour free mooring close to the staithe and mooring outside the riverside pubs for paying customers. Close to the staithe is also a pay and display car park for visitors arriving by road.

Horning Church

Distance: 4.6km (2.9 Miles)
Time: 1 Hour 30 Minutes
Parking: Staithe Car Park **NR12 8AA**

Starting at the Ferry Inn follow the track out to the road and turn right. Continue for 500m to the school and turn right. A further 500m will bring you to the parish church. Just on the other side of the church yard there is a permissive path leading you next to the vicarage and gently down to the River Bure and private moorings for the church. Continue back to the church yard and follow the footpath heading right along the field edge just on the north side of the church grounds. The path follows a line between two fields and at the end you will join a track next to a country lane. Turn right to follow the track south for 400m, gently down to the riverbank and another lookout over the River Bure.

After enjoying the view head back up the path to the road to the fork just by the path you came out at earlier. Take the left country lane which will lead you in a westerly direction. After 300m at the crossroads continue straight ahead and follow this country lane all the way back to the start of the walk.

Horning Church

Walk 15:
Alderfen Broad

Distance: 9.0km (5.6 Miles)
Time: 3 Hours
Parking: Staithe Car Park **NR12 8AA**

From the pay and display car park in Horning, follow the road away from the river and towards the main road. Cross the road and follow the lane opposite for 220m where there is a public footpath crossing the field diagonally on the right. Follow this path until you reach the road at RAF Neatishead. Turn right and follow the lane for a little over 500m to the first road on the left. Turn left and follow the lane north for 900m to Threehammer Common. As you enter the small cluster of houses there is a long straight track on the right after the last house on the right. Follow this to Alderfen Broad nature reserve. Visit the Alderfen Broad page in the Irstead chapter for further details (page 80). Turn right and follow the public footpath through the woodlands along the dyke. This is straight to begin with and then twists and turns close to the southern end of the broad before appearing out at a country lane.

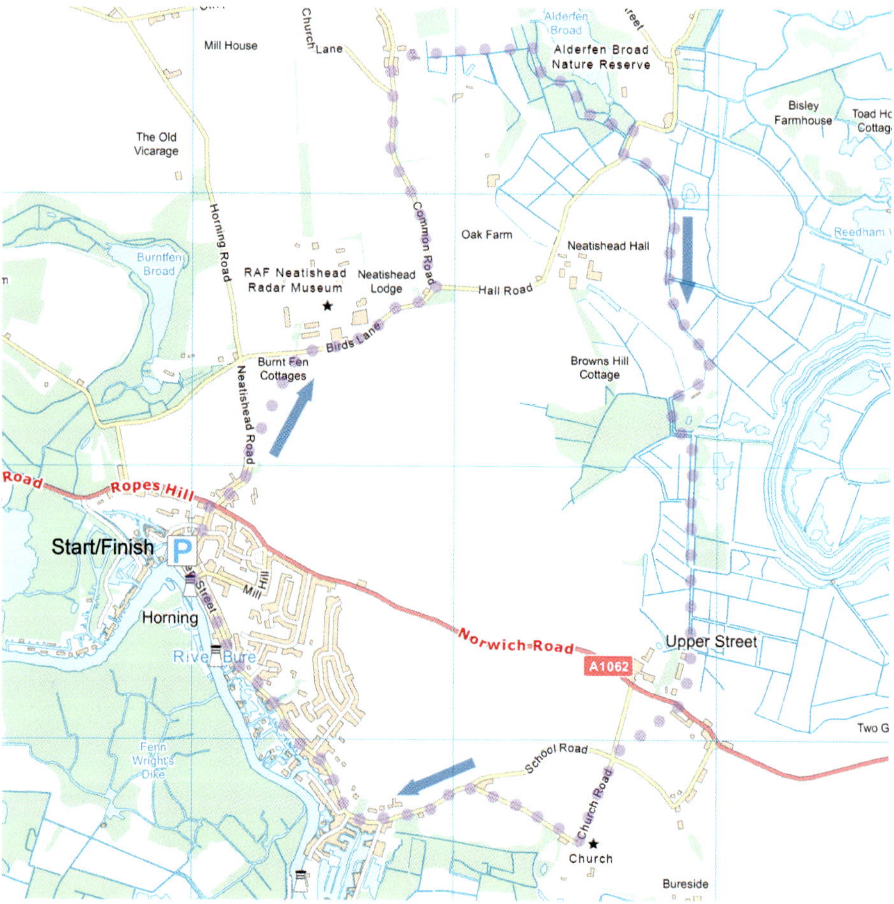

At the lane turn right and follow the road south for 125m to a public footpath on the left down a private driveway. Follow the public footpath along the drive as it heads south. After 950m you will arrive at a couple of houses, here the path heads right and into a small wood. The path turns left and follows a dyke and then turns left up to a private boat house on the other side of the footbridge. Just before the boathouse the footpath turns right and heads south in a straight line with a dyke on the right. Continue along this path as it joins a track and passes several houses at Horning Upper Street. Once you arrive at the road there is a public footpath opposite, take this along the edge of the property and then diagonally across the field to the road. At the road continue straight ahead towards the church just under 400m away. Follow the road sharply right at the church and continue 450m to the junction by the school. Turn left and follow this country lane back into Horning. The same road will lead you all the way back to the Staithe and parking area.

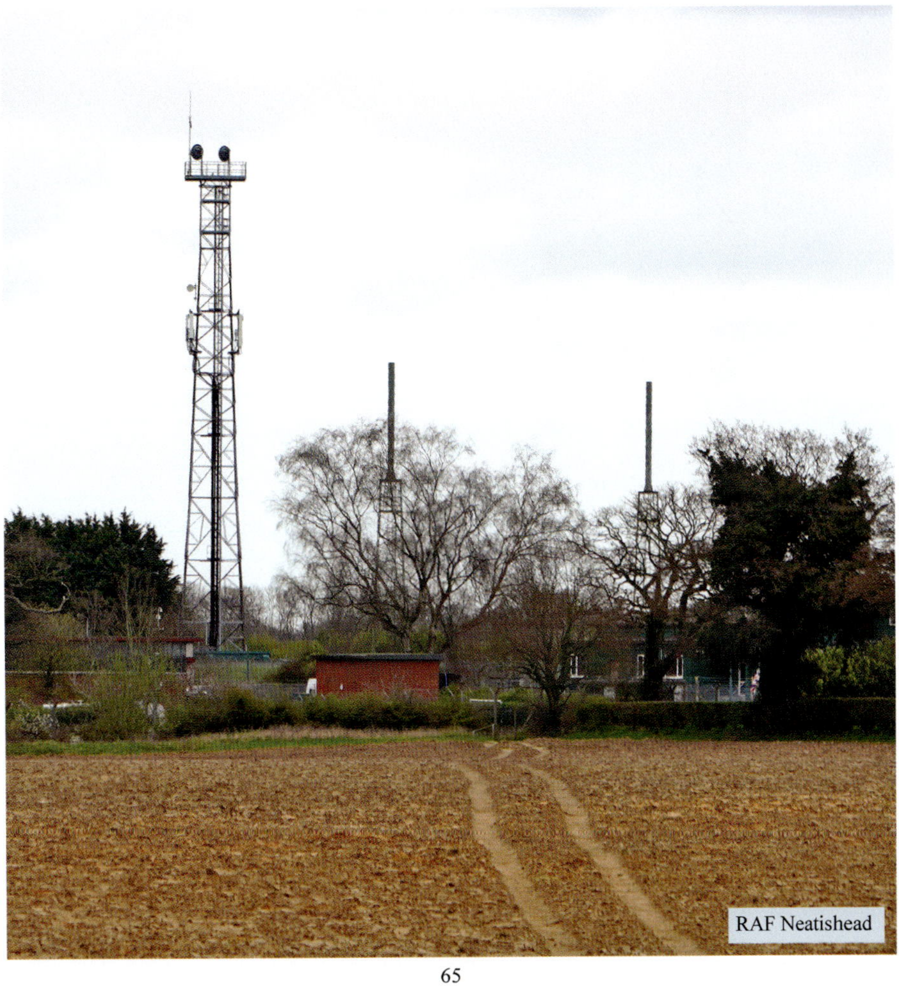

RAF Neatishead

Alderfen Broad and Barton Broad

Horsey

Meadow Dyke

Horsey

Horsey is a small rural village within walking distance from the coast. There are many activities to do here including boat trips onto Horsey Mere, walks through the Nature Reserve and to the sea and the ever popular Horsey Windpump. The village church of All Saints is situated just off the road through the village and has a rare round tower making it an interesting target to walk to. Another interesting feature of the surrounding landscape is Brograve Drainage Mill along Waxham Cut with its distinctive lean to one side. The large car park is owned by the National Trust providing free parking for members. Its worth noting that Horsey Mere is closed to boat traffic through the winter months.

Horsey Windpump

Horsey Windpump was bought by the National Trust in 1948 and protected with a Grade II* listing. It was originally constructed in the mid 19th Century but rebuilt in 1897 and then again in 1912. There is an entry fee but inside you can read about the history of the area and the mill as you work your way to the viewing platform at the top with views over to Somerton, Martham and Horsey Mere.

Walk 16:
Brograve Mill

Distance: 5.0km (3.1 Miles)
Time: 1 Hour 45 Minutes
Parking: Staithe Car Park **NR29 4EF**

From the National Trust car park by Horsey Staithe, head up to the dyke and turn right along the north side of the water's edge. After 120m the path turns to the right and continues about the same distance before bending round to the left. Continue to follow this footpath along the north side of Horsey Mere and then along Waxham Cut in a straight line until you reach the opposite side of the river to Brograve Drainage Mill. The mill can be seen for a good section of the walk, and although it is in ruins, it is quite a sight with the tower subsiding slightly. Turn right, away from the mill and dyke in a straight line towards a small wood. At the wood the path turns left then right and up to a narrow lane. Turn right here and after just a few metres turn left along the footpath which after about 200m turns right and heads south. The path eventually joins the narrow lane and continues to All Saints Church. Just beyond the church the road turns left and heads up to a junction. Turn right here and follow the path along the edge of the road back to Horsey Staithe.

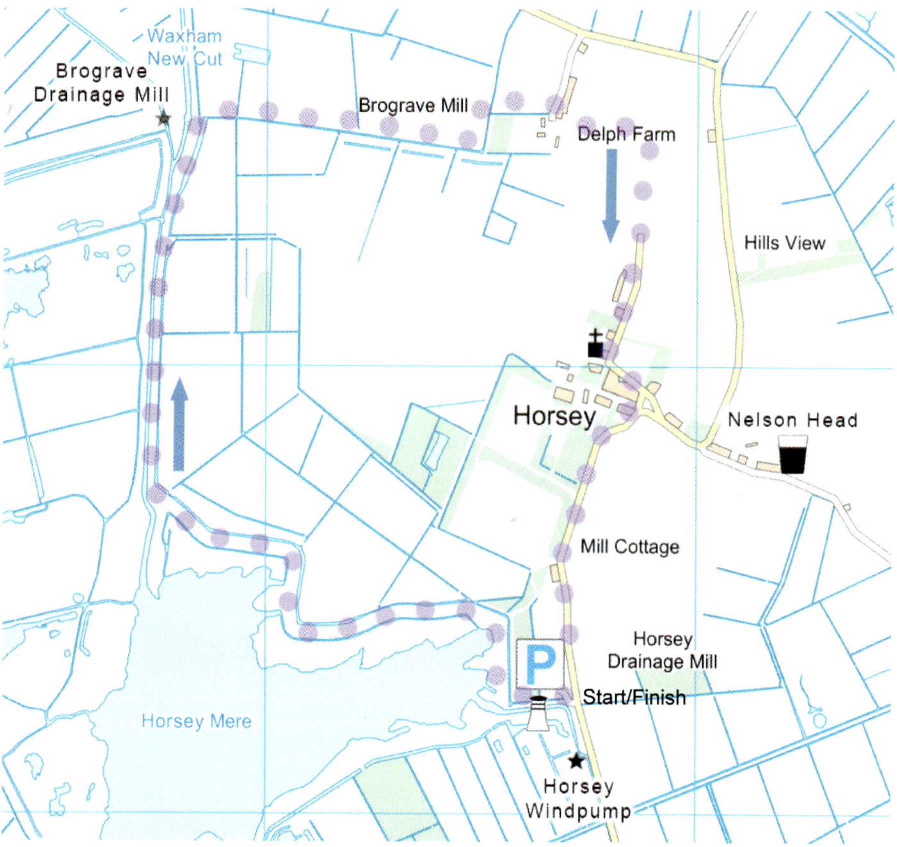

Brograve Drainage Mill

The leaning ruins of Brograve Drainage Mill are exceptionally picturesque and seen regularly on postcards for the area. The mill is believed to date to the early 19th Century and may have had the largest sails of any drainage mill in Norfolk!

Walk 17: Horsey Gap

Distance: 5.8km (3.6 Miles)
Time: 2 Hours
Parking: Staithe Car Park **NR29 4EF**

From the car park and staithe, head to the road and directly opposite the car park entrance is a permissive footpath heading east over a stile and along the field edge. After about 450m the path turns left to join a track that heads up to the road. Turn right and follow the road as it turns into a rough track north east and after about 1.2km arrives at the dunes overlooking the beach. There is a choice here of either following the shoreline or dune path, but whichever you choose to do, turn left and follow the coast for 1.2km (¾ of a mile) to Horsey Gap where you will encounter a car park and optional start for this walk. Turn left and follow the access road for the car park which leads south west and up to the coast road. Turn right and just over 100m turn left along the footpath down the field edge towards a line of trees. The path continues straight ahead to eventually join the country lane

leading to the Church of All Saints. Just past the church turn left and follow the lane up to the junction and turn right. Follow the roadside path back to the staithe and parking.

Horsey Gap

Church of All Saints, Horsey

The Church of All Saints in Horsey is one of only 124 round tower churches in the county and largely dates to the 13th Century. It was restored in 1855 and now protected with a Grade II* listing.

Irstead

River Ant

Irstead

Irstead is quietly tucked away about 3 miles north of Ludham Bridge along the River Ant. Its location makes it surrounded by stunning waterways and areas of wild natural beauty. Only a 20 minute stroll from the staithe at Irstead is the Irstead Boardwalk, a purpose built route that takes walkers through a small section of nature reserve to a viewing platform overlooking Barton Broad. This area is becoming well known for its wildlife, ranging from Marsh Harriers and Otters, to Treecreepers and Reed Warblers. Alternatively, about 25 minutes away is Alderfen National Nature Reserve managed by the Norfolk Wildlife Trust. The Reserve is one of Norfolk's hidden treasures, being tucked away in dense woodland and surrounded by farmland. The reserve consists of open water, reedbed, marsh and woodland with several meandering paths leading you through this mosaic habitat. A small viewing screen is an excellent place to watch the rippling waters trying to spot something special. The village is so small that it lacks a village shop or pub, the nearest being a couple of miles down the road at either Neatishead or Horning. There is free mooring and parking available at the staithe.

Walk 18: Irstead Boardwalk

Distance: 2.9km (1.8 Miles)
Time: 1 Hour 30 Minutes
Parking: Staithe Car Park **NR12 8XS**

From the car park at the staithe follow the country lane alongside the attractive 15th Century church of St. Michael. About 400m past the parish church is a country lane on the right. Turn down this road which passes a small post box on the left and continues straight for 200m before turning sharply left. Continue another 250m. On the right will be a small car park for disabled visitors to the boardwalk. Join the boardwalk on the other side of the car park and begin to follow it round. At the split you can either turn left or right, my personal preference is to keep right and continue round to the viewing platform first and enjoying a longer stroll round the reserve afterwards. At the next split turn right to head to the viewing platform over Barton Broad. Once you have enjoyed the view over the broad backtrack to the split and turn right, follow the walk around the reserve taking the left path at the next split. This will lead you back to the small car park and then retrace your steps back to the staithe.

Barton Broad Viewpoint

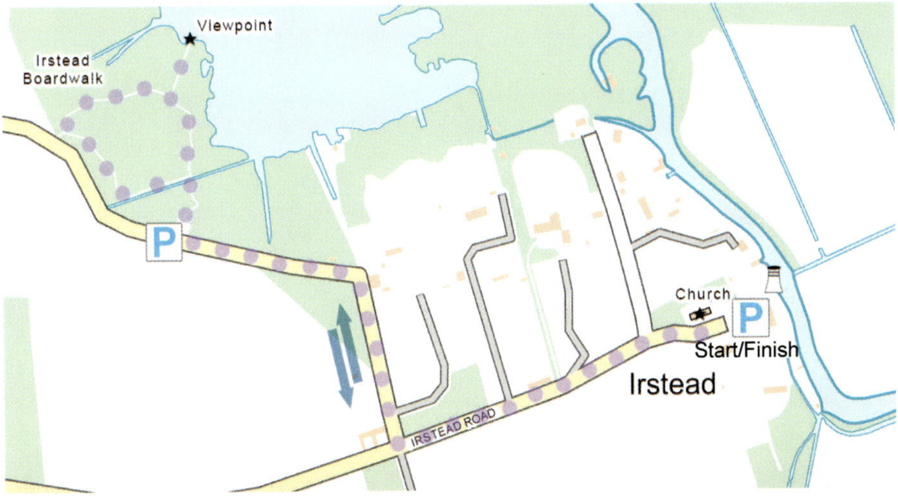

Bluebells at Irstead

Irstead Boardwalk

Walk 19: Alderfen Broad

Distance: 7.3km (4.5 Miles)
Time: 3 Hours
Parking: Staithe Car Park **NR12 8XS**

From the car park at the staithe follow the country lane past St. Michael's Church for about 600m and take the first road on the left. Continue down this lane for 1km (0.6 Miles) where it turns sharply right near Irstead Street. Shortly after this bend in the road there is a further bend to the left. Just at this sharp turn left there is a public footpath leading into Alderfen on the right (not to be confused with the track on the right just before the footpath). The start of this section is through dense woodland and after a short distance it follows a dyke all the way to the main entrance to the reserve. Take some time here to look around the ancient woodlands and stroll to the viewing platform near the entrance. An information board is located here showing reserve paths.

Alderfen Broad Nature Reserve

Alderfen Broad is a 53 acre Site of Special Scientific Interest (SSSI) close to the River Ant and Barton Broad. Being isolated from the main waterways of the Norfolk Broads, this small body of water is a tranquil and quiet place with no motor crafts and plenty of wildlife to see including Kingfishers, Marsh Harriers and numerous insects and invertebrates. The site is owned and managed by Norfolk Wildlife Trust and free to explore.

Alderfen Broad

Leave the Nature Reserve by the trackway at the main entrance. Follow the track for about 220m, keeping an eye out for another track on the right. Follow this second track in a straight line for 300m where it turns sharply left onto a footpath alongside another field. Look for the public footpath on the right after 70m which runs alongside fencing and housing and ends up at a small country lane. On arrival at the lane, turn left, follow it for 100m and turn left again. Continue down this road for about 200m where the road turns sharply left. Do not follow the road to the left, instead follow the track on the right (like a driveway) with lovely houses on either side, all the way to the footpath at the end. Follow this public footpath through the nearby fields, keeping an eye out for the footpath on the right dividing the field and heading up in the direction of the plantation on the top of the hill. The footpath ends on a small road where you need to turn right and then follow the first footpath on the left. This will take you diagonally across the field and end at a road. Turn left and follow this road back into Irstead.

Alderfen Broad

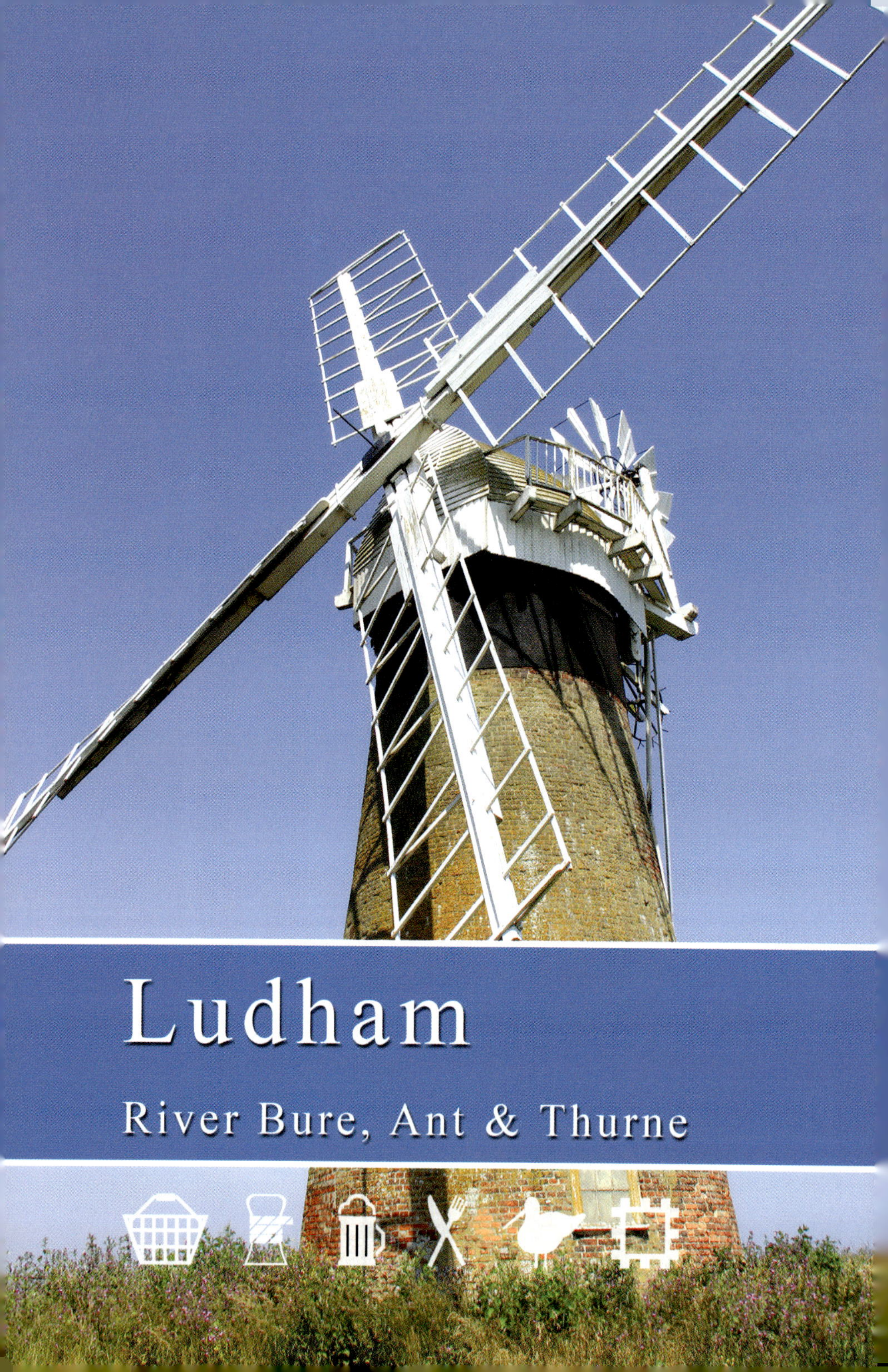

Ludham

River Bure, Ant & Thurne

Ludham

Ludham is a small village, easily accessible by car via the A1062 and by boat thanks to it being surrounded by river on three sides. There is free parking in the village just by the church and free mooring at four points along the river, these are Womack Water, St Benet's Abbey, Ludham Bridge and How Hill. The village has two pubs, The Dog Inn by Ludham Bridge and the Kings Head in the village centre with Throwers convenience store opposite and small team room by the church. Surrounding Ludham are several nature reserves with Womack Marshes to the south east, How Hill Fen by Ludham Bridge and then just to the north west is How Hill and Crome's Broad. How Hill is a stunning visitor attraction with small museum and nature trails through the marshes and woodland. South of the village is one of the most famous sites on the Broads with the ruins of St Benet's Abbey adorning many postcards and book covers.

Below is a map of Ludham Bridge, approximately 1 mile from the main village but still regarded as Ludham. Parking here is available in the lay-bys and 24 Hour free mooring along the River Ant.

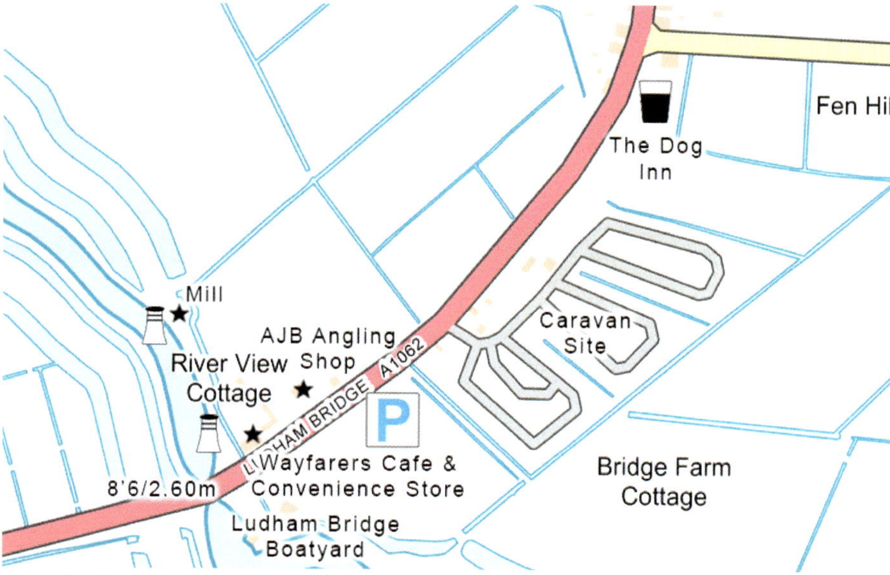

Ludham Bridge

How Hill

How Hill is a beautiful place for a short walk along the river or longer visit exploring the meandering paths through the marsh and woodland. There are several bird hides overlooking the most wildlife rich areas including a scrape close to the river and Crome's Broad. The tiny Marshman's Cottage known as Toad Hole Cottage just by the entrance to the reserve is a museum detailing the life of locals in the early 1900s. Boat trips are available taking visitors along parts of the River Ant and between the reedbeds to an isolated bird hide overlooking Reedham Water. The main house in the estate dates back to 1904 and is now used as a study centre for school visits.

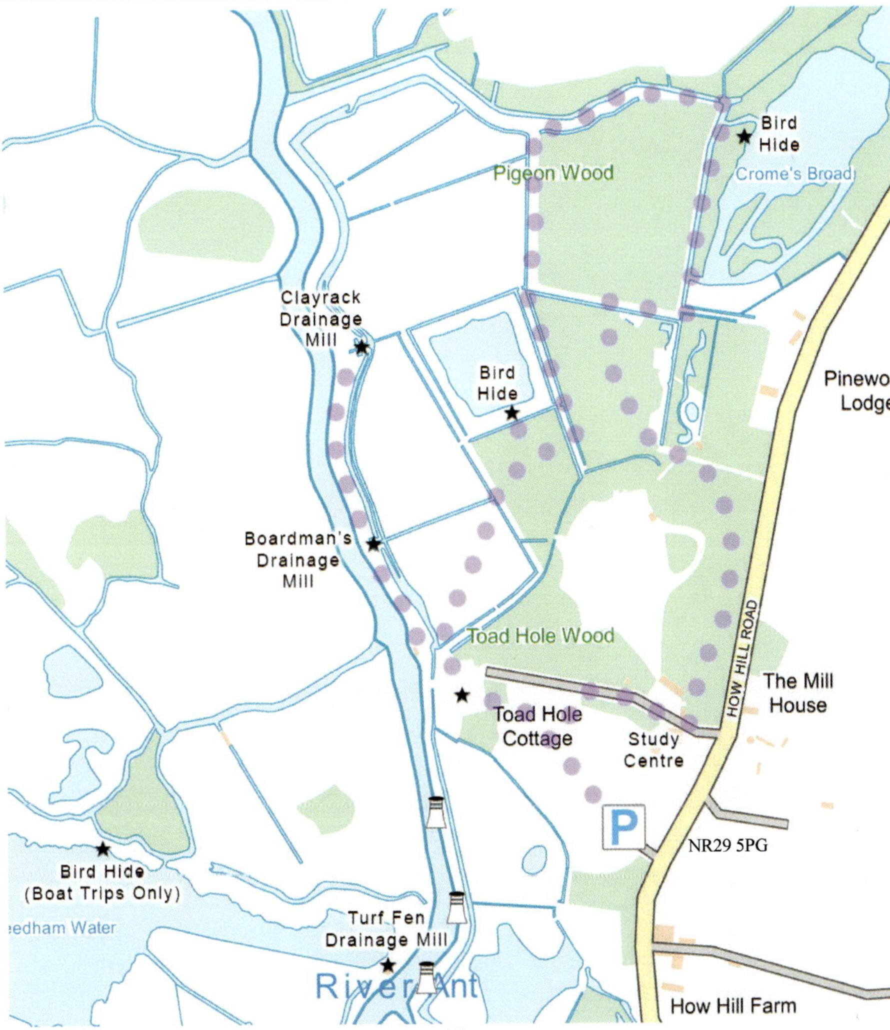

Turf Fen Drainage Mill

Just south of How Hill along the River Ant is Turf Fen Drainage Mill. It was built in 1880 to drain Horning Marshes but ceased working in the 1920s and has been given a Grade II* listing.

Boardman's Skeleton Mill

Boardman's Skeleton Mill

Boardman's Drainage Mill at How Hill was built in 1897 by a local millwright and is now a Grade II* listed building. This Trestle mill is one of only three remaining skeleton mills on The Broads.

Turf Fen Drainage Mill

St Benet's Abbey

St Benet's Abbey was founded in 1020AD and rose to be one of the wealthiest Benedictine houses in the country. It was also the only Anglo-Saxon monastery in the country which continued in use throughout the Middle-Ages, and the only monastery to survive the Dissolution by King Henry VIII. Sadly not much remains now because in the sixteenth century all of the buildings except the gatehouse were demolished. When taking a walk around the site keep an eye out for the noticeable earthworks and the stone remains of some of the buildings. The easiest to recognise is the abbey church sitting on a slight mound above the marshes. Some of the exterior walls have superb flint work and inside the mill the preservation of the arches and stone carvings is fantastic. The mill was built in the 18th Century on top of the gatehouse ruins and during thr construction, builders destroyed the second floor of the gatehouse. The small gravel island the abbey was built on is known as Cow Holm and visitors are free to walk around the precinct to view the remnants of this once thriving religious area.

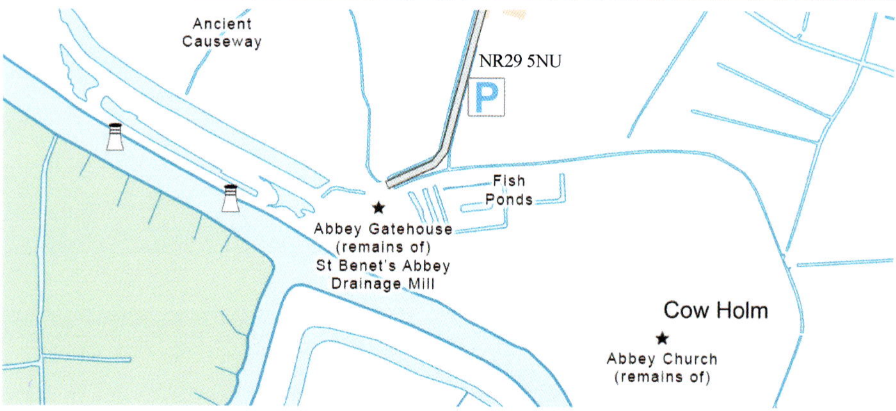

The Oak Cross, St Benet's Abbey

Walk 20:
How Hill Fen

Distance: 5.2km (3.2 Miles)
Time: 1 Hour 30 Minutes
Parking: Roadside Layby **NR29 5NX**

From the free moorings and car park at Ludham Bridge head past the cafe and in the direction of The Dog Inn. Continue past The Dog Inn up to the end of the houses. Safely follow the road for about 300m where there will be a farm on your left. Follow the lane through the farm which will end at a gate by The Limes and change into a trackway. Head along the track as it turns into a regular footpath with open fields to the right and a hedge-line on the left. The path will come to a gate and turn sharply right through the reeds. Look out for the first footpath on the left after 300m and once at the footpath, follow it to a raised bank. Climb the steep bank and turn left and continue to follow the raised bank all the way back to Ludham Bridge (approximately 2.5km) keeping an eye out for any of the wildlife in the pools alongside.

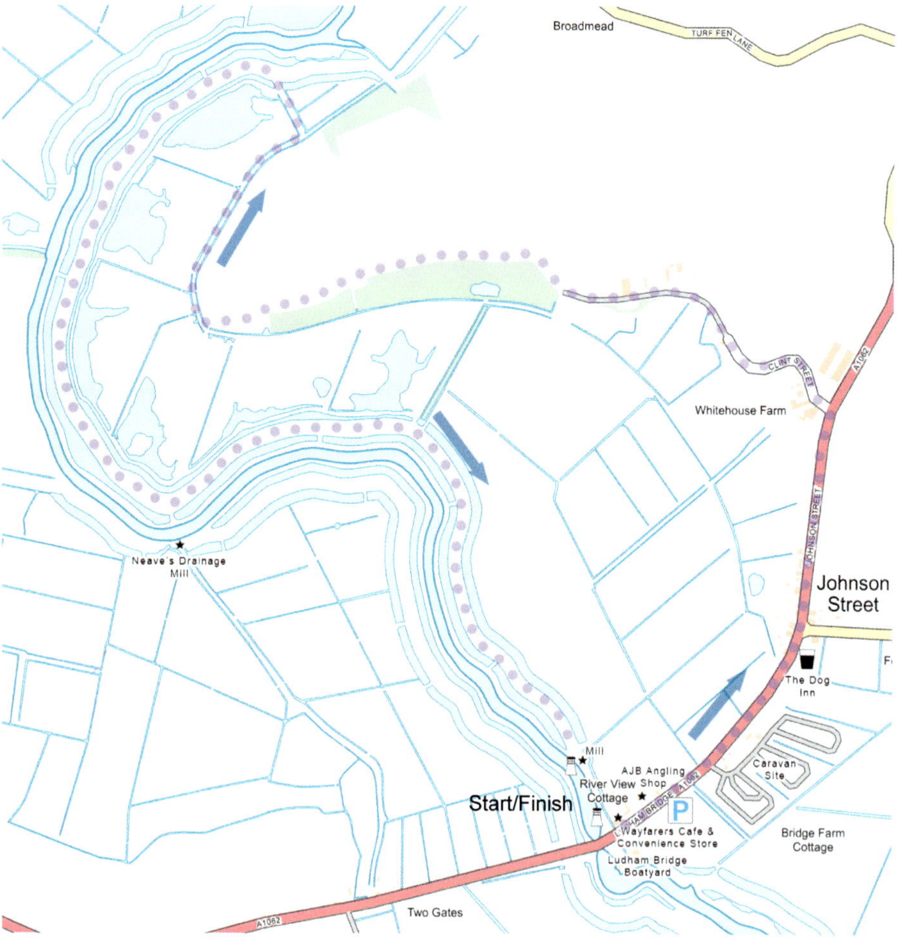

Ludham Bridge Drainage Mill

Ludham Bridge Drainage Mill is an easy feature to identify standing only 20ft high and with its distinctive lean. It is located just north of the bridge along the east side of the riverbank and it is quite interesting to note that the base was once used as a pill box!

Neave's Drainage Mill

Neave's Drainage Mill is a 4 storey tower mill that was built in 1870. It sits just on the western side of the River Ant north of Ludham Bridge and is given a Grade II listing.

Walk 21:
Womack Marshes

Distance: 5.2km (3.2 Miles)
Time: 2 Hours
Parking: Staithe Car Park **NR29 5QG**

From the moorings and car park at Womack Staithe turn right to follow Horse Fen Road south east. Follow the road until its end at Hunters Yard where it turns into a track that heads off to the left. Don't follow the track past the cottage, instead follow the footpath directly in front which runs alongside Hunters Yard and parallel to Womack Water. Continue to follow the path down along Womack Water to the point where it joins the River Thurne and bends around to the left, following the River Thurne for 1km. At the end of this riverbank path the route crosses a metal bridge next to a pumping station and joins a long straight trackway. Follow the trackway North West away from the river for 500m where it bends round to the right and continues straight for another 250m. The track then bends round to the left to join a small country lane leading into the tiny hamlet of Fritton. After 600m, opposite a house called Fritton Thatch is a public bridleway lined by bushes and then opens out to follow the edge of some fields. The path then joins a track that continues in a straight line to finally join the main road. Follow the road left and left again to follow the small country lane back down to Womack Staithe.

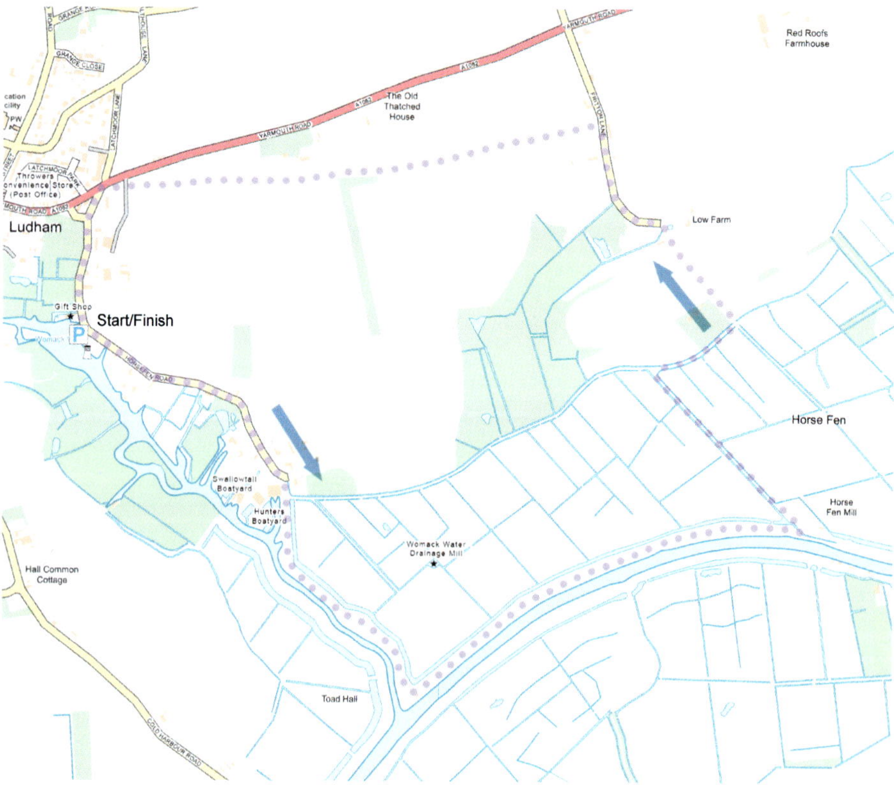

Womack Water Drainage Mill

Womack Water Drainage Mill is a small 3 storey red brick mill that can be seen along the entire riverbank section of the walk. Its original height was about 23 feet.

Walk 22: Ludham Hall

Distance: 5.3km (3.3 Miles)
Time: 2 Hours
Parking: Roadside Layby **NR29 5NX**

From Ludham Bridge, with the small shop and café on your left, follow the road away from the bridge and past The Dog Inn to the first road on the right. Turn right to follow this small country lane for 500m to the driveway of Ludham Hall which can be seen over to the left most of the way along the road. Head down the driveway, past the hall and along the track out the other side. This track continues for 700m until it joins another track called Lovers Lane. Turn left to follow Lovers Lane north towards the main village of Ludham. On arrival at the main road turn right to follow the path alongside the road to avoid the traffic and continue up to the church. Just past the church is a road off to the right. Follow this past the doctors surgery and all the way down to the road heading off to the right about 900m away (Hall Common Road). Follow this country lane on the right for 1.4km past Ludham Hall and to the main road where you need to turn left to head back to Ludham Bridge.

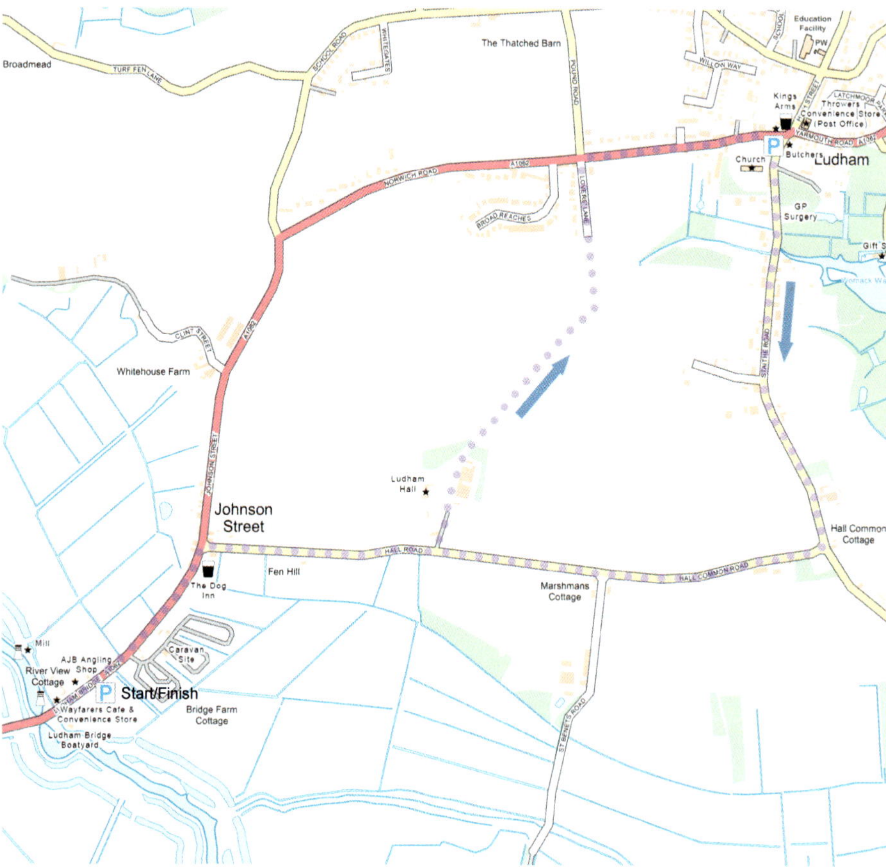

Ludham Church

Ludham Hall

The stunning Grade II* listed house of Ludham Hall was built on the site of a Bishop's Palace which burnt down in 1611. The current building is 18th Century but incorporates parts of the older structure. A chapel stands at a right angle to the hall and dates to around the same period and now used as a barn.

Ludham Hall and Chapel

Martham

River Thurne

Martham

Martham is a large village within the Thurne valley offering a selection of pubs, shops and takeaways. Parking is available in the village centre but mooring can be a little tricky as there are no Broads Authority moorings along the River Thurne at Martham, the nearest being at Potter Heigham or Somerton roughly 2 miles away. On the north side of the village is the Norfolk Wildlife Trust Martham Broad Nature Reserve, home to rare species like Bittern and Marsh Harrier. Just west of here is the National Trust Heigham Holmes nature reserve which is accessed via a ferry and open at selected times of the year. The site is home to numerous species of Owl and also breeding Cranes.

St Mary's Church, Martham

The parish church of St Mary is a lovely Grade I listed building that dates to the late 14th Century. The tower, complete with a small spire on the top soars above the surrounding marsh at 98ft tall and can be seen for miles around.

Walk 23: River Thurne

Distance: 5.7km (3.5 Miles)
Time: 2 Hours
Parking: Roadside **NR29 4PA**

from the village green, head west over towards the Co-op foodstore and head north down Black Street opposite. The road eventually passes the large parish church and at the sharp bend, turn left along Staithe Road. Just ahead is a sharp bend in the road, here take the track on the left and follow it round to the right and towards the farm on Thunder Hill. The path passes through the farm and out the other side along the edge of the field to a corner. The path crosses the field to the west and up to a boundary and along the field edge to the road. Turn right and follow the road to the end where it will arrive at a boatyard and the River Thurne. Follow the River Thurne on the right behind a series of waterside properties and up to Martham Level Drainage Mill. The path continues past the mill and up to Martham Ferry and another dyke. Follow the path round to the right along the dyke and up to the road which is followed back into the village of Martham. At the sharp bend follow the road round to the left and up to the junction. Turn right past the church and back to the village green.

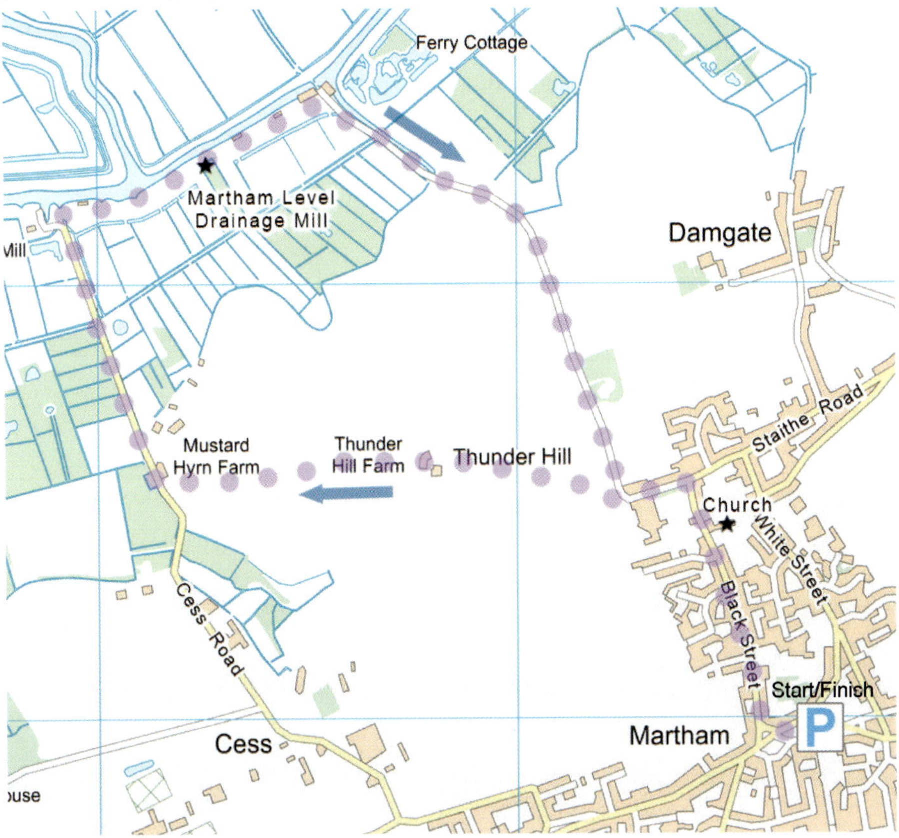

Marshes around Martham

Martham Level Drainage Mill

Martham Level Drainage Mill dates to 1908 and sits close to the River Thurne at a split with Candle Dyke heading north west and the River Thurne continuing north east. The Grade II building has now been converted into a dwelling, preserving it for generations to come.

Walk 24:
Martham Broad

Distance: 8.8km (5.5 Miles)
Time: 3 Hours
Parking: Roadside **NR29 4PA**

This walk may also be started from moorings close to Martham Broad or Somerton Staithe.

From Martham Green follow the road west past the duck pond and towards the Coop Supermarket. Opposite the shop is Black Street which heads north towards the Parish Church and to a sharp bend round to the right. Take the road on the left at this bend (Staithe Road) and follow the lane all the way to the boat dyke. Once at the dyke bear right along the right hand side of the moorings where the path passes a small car park for the fishing lakes and then along the riverbank round to the right. On the opposite bank is Heigham Holmes Nature Reserve, owned and managed by the National Trust. The riverbank is followed for 1.3km to a bend round to the right and past a small area of mooring which is an optional start point if arriving by boat. The path heads south and then follows a gentle curve round to the left, around the south side of Martham Broad Nature Reserve and enters a small area of woodland. As you reach the end of the woodland the path follows the edge of the vast reedbed to the east and eventually reaches the River Thurne again at Somerton Dyke. The dyke is followed until you reach the country lane and then turn right for a short way, gently bending left and then right and up to a country lane. Turn left along Sandy Lane and take the footpath across the field on the right just before the first country lane on your left. Stick to the well defined track between the fields and after about 1km the track joins a country lane just past some houses and has entered the village of Damgate just to the north east of Martham.

Martham Broad

Bear left and follow Damgate Back Lane south where it turns into a track and gently curves round to the main road. Turn right along the pavement and at the fork just ahead bear right onto Staithe Road. Take the first road on the left (School Road) and then at the junction bear right round past the church and stick to this road as it heads back to the village green.

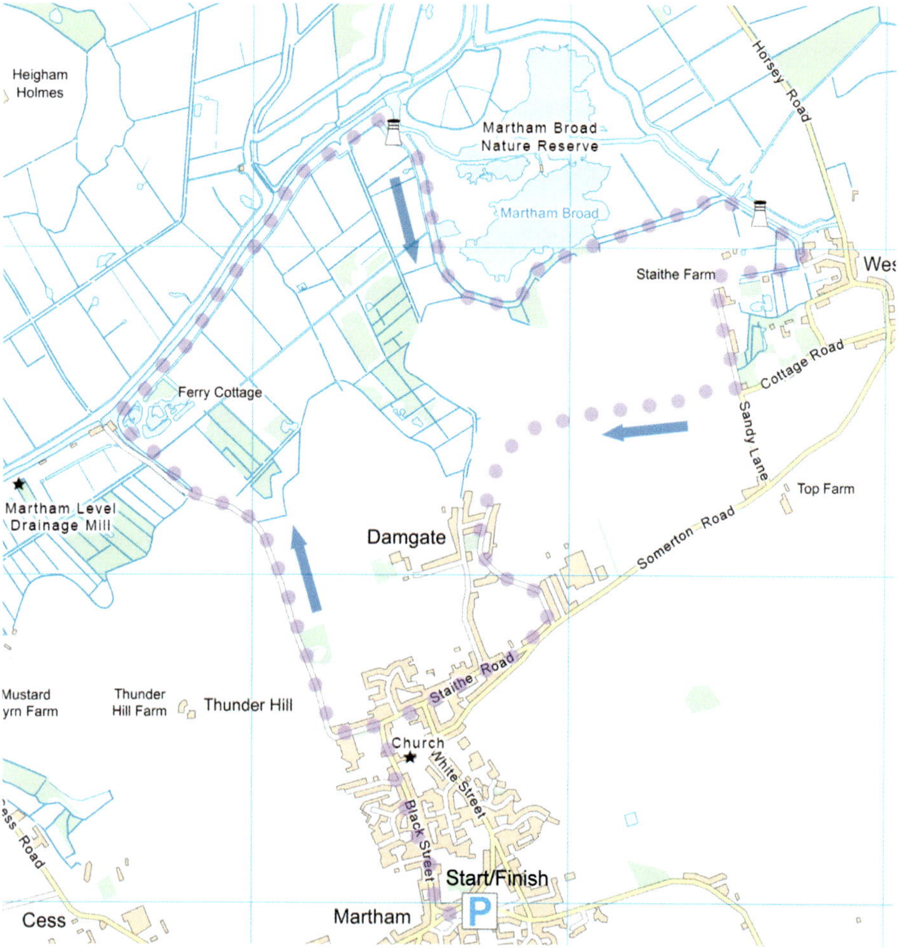

Heigham Holmes

Heigham Holmes is a large isolated island owned and managed by the National Trust and surrounded by river, broad and marsh. The site was operated as a farm for many years before being turned into a nature reserve that allows the general public to explore only one day each year. Access to the reserve is over an unusual floating swing bridge called Martham Ferry on its opening days and is home to incredibly rare breeding Cranes, numerous species of Owl and other farmland birds.

Neatishead

River Ant

Neatishead

Neatishead is a small village just a couple of miles north of Horning and close to Barton Turf on the edge of Barton Broad. Mooring is available along Limekiln Dyke at the public staithe and at Gaye's Staithe with a small car park just to the south of here for visitors arriving by car. The White Horse Inn sits in the heart of the village opposite a small community shop selling all the essentials. One of the local attractions is the Barton Broad Boardwalk which takes walkers to a viewing platform overlooking the massive expanse of Barton Broad. The boardwalk is covered more in the Irstead chapter but a walk there is included from Gaye's Staithe.

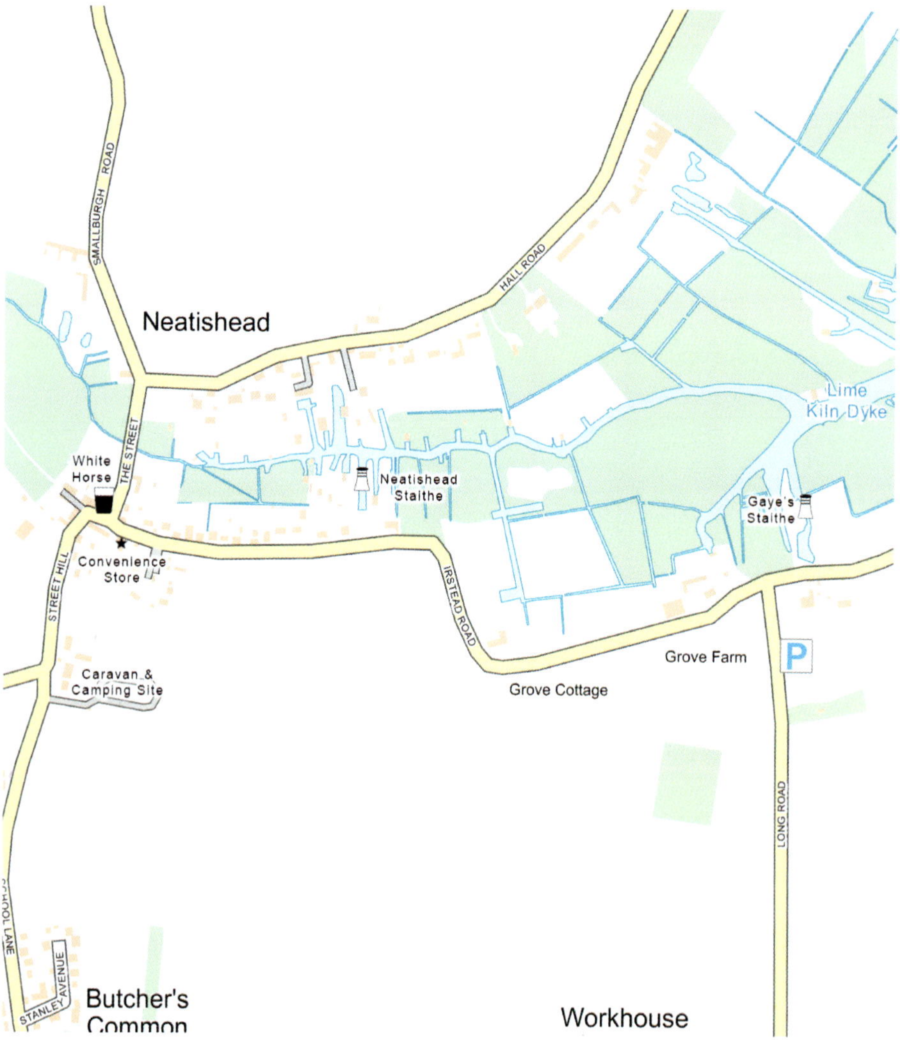

Walk 25:
Irstead Boardwalk

Distance: 2.7km (1.7 Miles)
Time: 1 Hour
Parking: Broad Car Park **NR12 8XP**

From Gaye's Staithe head along the access track to the road and turn right, taking the first road on the left past the car park (start here if parking in the car park). Just beyond the car park is a small wood on the left, follow the path round the left hand side of it which heads east along a hedge and up to the road. Follow the road straight ahead for just over 600m to the main entrance to the boardwalk which provides disabled parking. Follow the boardwalk round to the viewpoint and back to the road. Once at the road turn right and follow it back to Gaye's Staithe.

Gayes Staithe

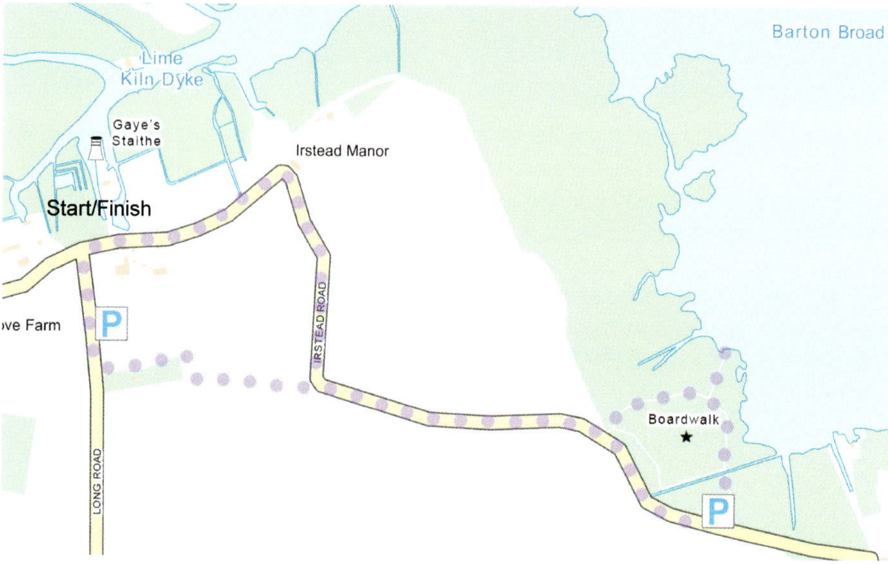

Irstead Boardwalk

Potter Heigham

River Thurne

Potter Heigham

Potter Heigham is a beautiful small village located along the River Thurne and famous for its large department store and its medieval stone bridge. The village is split into two halves, divided by the A149 main road, with a majority of the 1,000 strong population living on its northern side. The village hall, playground and church are all located on this side and within easy walking distance of the Staithe. There are a selection of interesting listed buildings in the village including the Grade I listed church of St Nicholas which dates to the 12th Century and of course the iconic stone bridge. Close to the staithe is a fantastic little cafe open throughout the year serving tasty home cooked food and a nearby fish & chip shop on the other side of the river. Thousands flock to the large discount department store of Lathams which has been on the site since the 1960s. Surrounding the village is low lying marsh surrounded by waterways, with Hickling Broad to the north, Heigham Sound to the east and the River Thurne to the south. This abundance of water invites in all kinds of wildlife which can be seen from the riverbank footpaths around the village.

Potter Heigham Bridge

The iconic Potter Heigham Bridge is famous for being one of the most difficult bridges to navigate in the entire national park and so has a bridge pilot service alongside for holiday cruisers. The bridge dates to the 14th Century with alterations in the 15th and late 18th Centuries and now protected as a Grade II* listed building and scheduled ancient monument.

St Nicholas Church, Potter Heigham

The lovely Grade I listed church of St Nicholas is by far the oldest building in the village and dates back to the 12th Century. The church is one of only 124 in the county with a round tower which is also the oldest part of the building.

Walk 26:
Horse Fen

Distance: 4.5km (2.8 Miles)
Time: 1 Hour 30 Minutes
Parking: Car Park **NR29 5JD**

From Potter Heigham Staithe, follow the path past Lathams Fishing Store and along the boat dyke to the river. The path follows the river south west, over a footbridge and then behind the riverside chalets. After about 900m a footpath turns off to the right along a line of trees and meanders its way through them until it reaches the edge of a field 800m away. Once at the open field turn right and follow it for about 150m where it bends to the right and follow the field edge north east with woodland up ahead. The path follows the edge of the wood for 250m before turning right and passing through the woodland to the east. The footpath eventually arrives at Mill Road with the tower mill just to the right. Turn left heading north along Mill Road and at the junction with the A1092 turn right and cross over the road to the shop. Follow the road right (Bridge Road) until you arrive back at Potter Heigham Staithe.

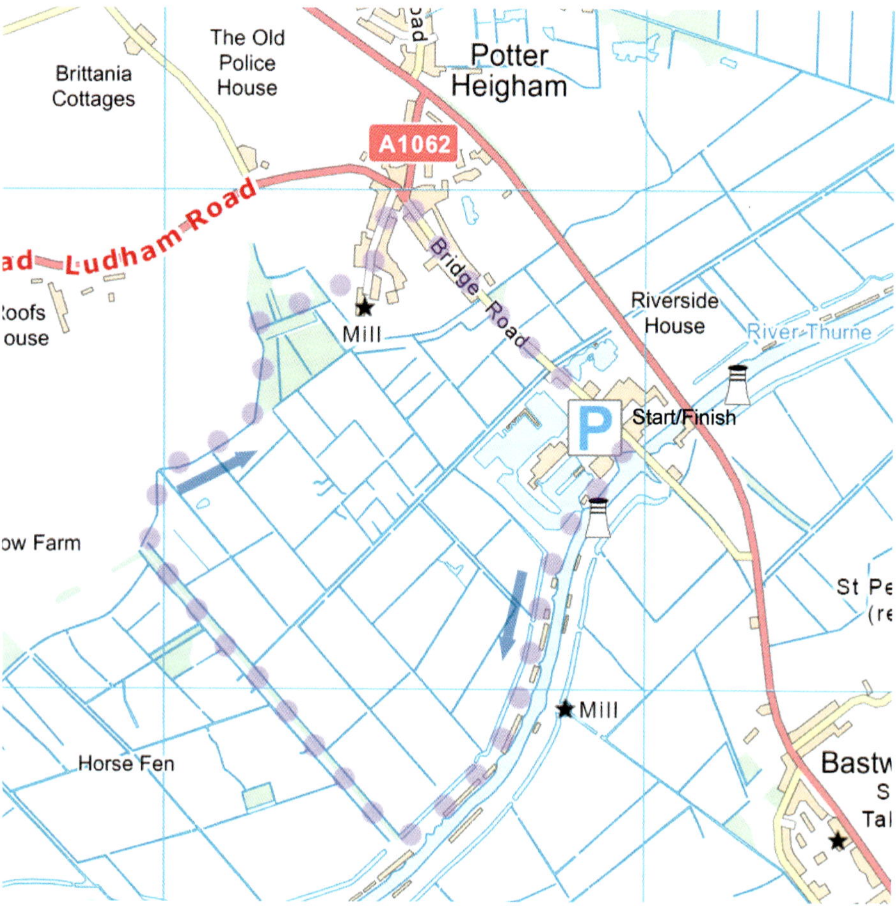

Sunways Mill

The large mill that can be seen just set back from the marshes around Horse Fen is called Sunways Mill and dates to 1849. It stands at a height of 6 storeys and protected as a grade II listed building.

Walk 27: Repps Staithe	
	Distance: 4.5km (2.8 Miles) **Time:** 1 Hour 30 Minutes **Parking:** Car Park **NR29 5JD**

From Potter Heigham Staithe, cross the medieval bridge towards the Fish and Chip Shop and just opposite the takeaway there is a footpath on the right along the driveway for Phoenix Fleet day boat hire. The path joins the riverbank and follows this to the south west, behind the riverside chalets and past a drainage mill. Eventually the path arrives at Repps Staithe and the road. Turn left along the lane and follow it past the small caravan park and Wind Energy Museum and just after the farm look out for a footpath on the left. Take the path across the field on the left in a straight line which passes a ruined barn and follows the edge of the fields in a gentle curve to arrive at the road in Repps. Turn left and after about 180m there is a footpath on the right leading to the Main Road next to the petrol station and convenience store. Turn left following the pavement along the A149 out of the village and at the split bear left (down Bridge Road) towards Potter Heigham Bridge and the staithe.

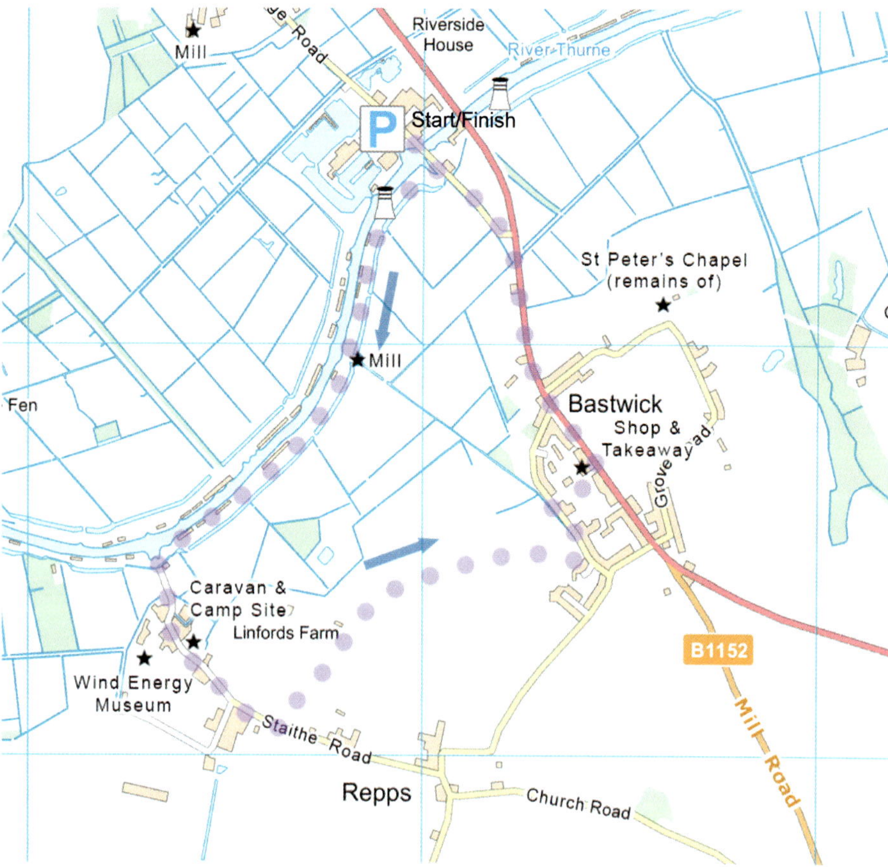

Repps Drainage Mill

Repps Level Drainage Mill sits not too far from Repps Staithe and probably dates to the late 19th Century. At the end of its working life it was converted into a dwelling in the 1970s.

Walk 28:
Hickling Broad

Distance: 10.0km (6.3 Miles)
Time: 3 Hours 30 Minutes
Parking: Car Park **NR29 5JD**

From Potter Heigham Bridge follow the riverbank path next to BridgeStones Cafe, signposted as the Weavers Way and the North Eastern Bank. The path passes a lovely grassed area before heading under the new road bridge and heading along a narrow concrete path behind the riverside chalets. At the end of the chalets the path briefly turns away from the river to pass under High's Drainage Mill and then a modern drainage pump before rejoining the riverbank. Just ahead the path passes a few more chalets and enters the new marshes and pools that were dug only a few years ago.

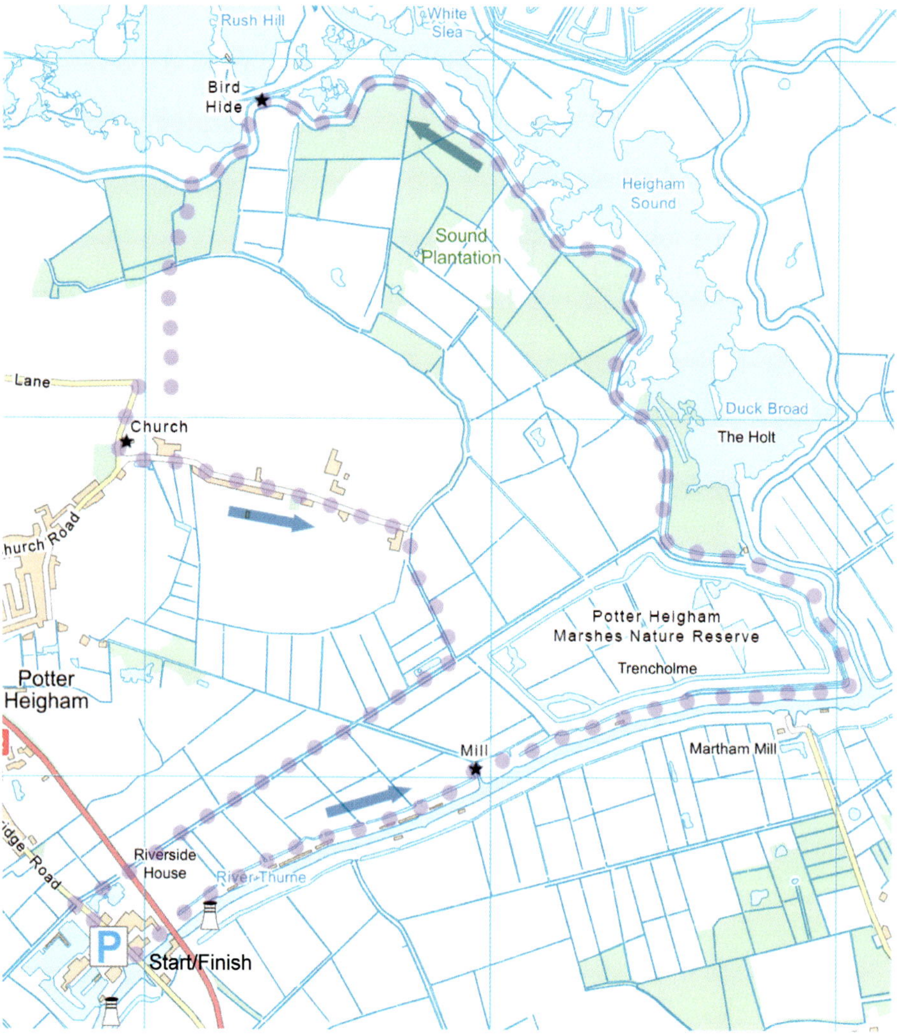

St Peter's Chapel Ruins

The ruins of St Peter's Chapel can be seen from the riverbanks around Potter Heigham and date back to the early 14th Century. The chapel was restored in 1905 but now ruined once again with only the tower surviving.

High's Drainage Mill

Highs Mill lies close to the River Thurne on its northern banks and dates to the mid 19th Century. The Grade II listed building is in good condition with a 4 storey tapering tower and boat shaped cap.

At the corner opposite Martham's riverside chalets the path turns left along a narrow river called Candle Dyke. Candle Dyke is a popular destination for fishermen and the likelihood is you will see someone along here. The path passes a small car park and sticks to the raised bank as it bends round to the north towards a small area of woodland. The wood is bypassed and another larger area of woodland is walked around with vast open reedbeds on the right and Heigham Sound just beyond. The path continues towards Hickling Broad past a small quay for the Boat Trips from the Norfolk Wildlife Trust Reserve and about 500m the Rush Hill Bird Hide is reached. After enjoying the view from the bird hide the path bends round to the left towards woodland and after 350m a public footpath heads off left into the wood.

Potter Heigham Marshes

Potter Heigham Marshes is a new area of wetland and reedbed made to replace lost habitat and increase the biodiversity of the area. The project has been extremely successful with a pair of Black Winged Stilts nesting in the reserve within the first couple of years. Although no hides overlook the scrapes, open water or reedbed, the riverbank path provides the best vantage points to see the interesting and rare wildlife living in the area.

Hickling Broad

Hickling Broad is the largest freshwater broad in Norfolk with restricted boat access to much of the water due to the depth being only 1.5m making it one of the best places to enjoy kayaking. A walk from Potter Heigham along the Weavers Way long distance path will lead to a bird hide overlooking Rush Hill, a watery scrape that attracts thousands of birds during the winter months. Access to other parts of the Broad can be walked from Hickling including many viewpoints from the Norfolk Wildlife Trust nature reserve.

This small area of woodland is known locally as Pickamore Woods and the path follows a ditch to the other side where the path turns left or right. Turn right and follow the path round to a straight line heading south towards Potter Heigham Church. Turn right at the track to the road and turn left up to the village church of St Nicholas. Turn left along Marsh Road in front of the church and follow the lane to the end of the road where the track splits by a farm. Keep right along the edge of the farm where the track follows a straight line to join another long straight track. Turn right here and stick to the straight track for 1.1km where it arrives at the A149 bypass. Cross carefully to the track on the other side and follow this to the next road, turning left and following the road back to Potter Heigham Staithe.

Ranworth

River Bure

Ranworth

Ranworth is an idyllic village with many interesting features and some basic facilities including a small village shop, tea rooms and The Maltsters pub. The staithe has free parking and mooring with additional mooring just across the other side of the Broad although take note that these additional moorings have no access to the village and are completely isolated. The village actually sits on the southern side of Malthouse Broad, named so from the old Maltings close to the village pub. Ranworth Broad just to the north west has no boat or car access, but walking there will lead you through a beautiful nature reserve to a floating visitor centre overlooking the water.

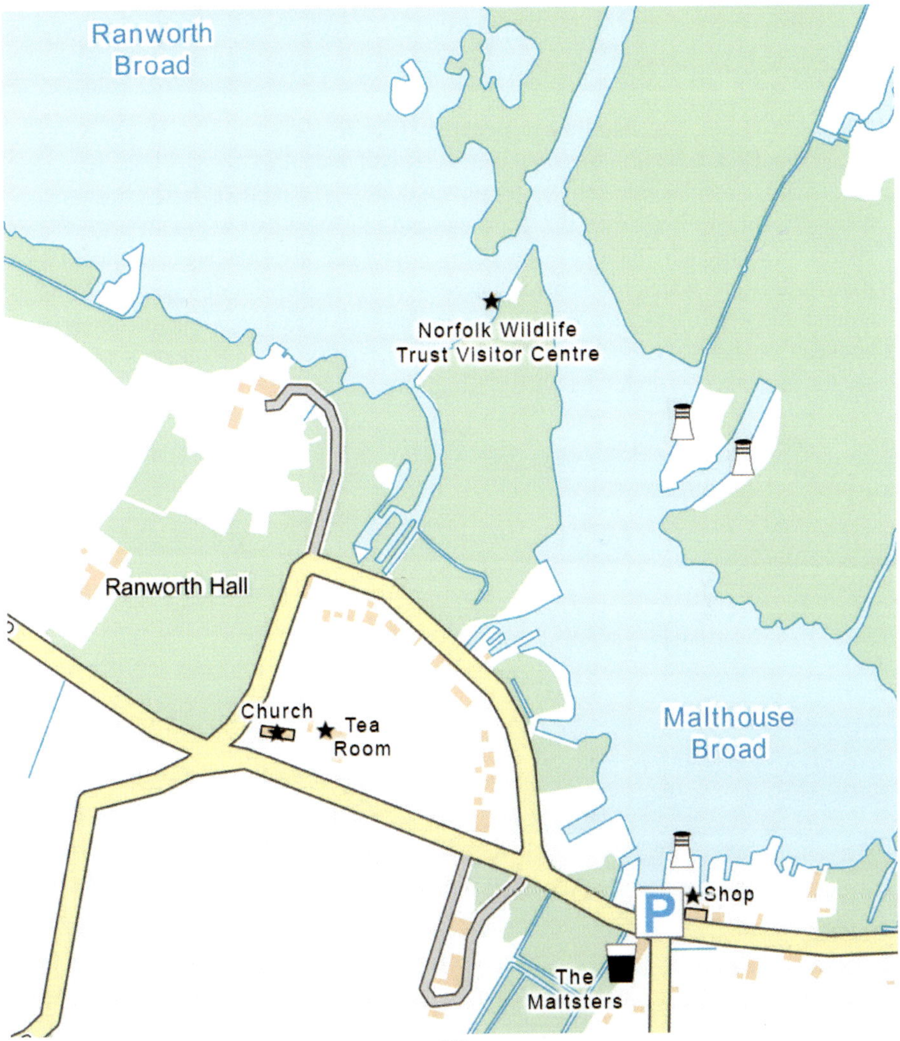

Ranworth Broad Nature Reserve

Ranworth Broad Nature Reserve is owned and managed by Norfolk Wildlife Trust and is an enjoyable activity for all the family. The floating visitor centre is a main attraction at Ranworth and sits at the end of almost half a mile of boardwalk taking you through ancient Alder Carr woodland and reedbed. It overlooks Ranworth Broad which has restricted access for boats allowing for peace and quiet around this wildlife sanctuary. Seasonal guided boat trips around the broad can be booked from here (subject to availability and times) giving you more opportunity to see the rarer species including Otters, Kingfishers and Marsh Harriers.

Walk 29:
Ranworth Broad

Distance: 1.7km (1.1 Miles)
Time: 1 Hour
Parking: Staithe Car Park **NR13 6HY**

From Ranworth Staithe head towards the Malsters pub and bear right along the roadside path which leads to a split in the road just ahead. Turn right down Broad Road and once past the moorings there is the entrance to the Norfolk Wildlife Trust Ranworth Broad Nature Reserve just on the right. Follow the path through the woodland and marshes until you reach the floating visitor centre. After spending some time here, follow the boardwalk back towards the road and at the split, keep right which leads to the country lane just ahead. Turn right and follow the lane round to the left past the village hall and up to the junction by the church and turn left again. If the church is open it's an absolute must to go inside and follow the spiral staircase to the viewpoint on the top of the tower (see page 118). Follow the road past the church which leads back to the staithe.

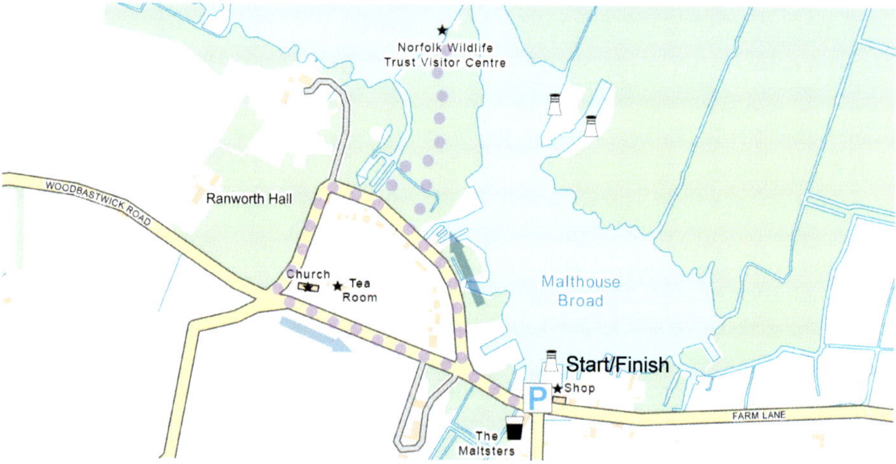

St Helen's Church, Ranworth

St Helen's Church is located a short walk from the Staithe and dates to 1370. The Church is referred to as The Cathedral of the Broads, and from the viewing platform at the top of the tower, the views extend for miles around. On a clear day it is apparently possible to see the spire on Norwich Cathedral over 8 miles away and the distinctive red and white striped Happisburgh Lighthouse 10 miles distant. Those with a keen eye may also make out the enigmatic remains of St Benet's Abbey on the other side of the River Bure near the village of Ludham. Legend has it that an underground tunnel once connected Ranworth Church with the Abbey.

Walk 30:
Ranworth Countryside

Distance: 2.5km (1.6 Miles)
Time: 1 Hour
Parking: Staithe Car Park **NR13 6HY**

With Malthouse Broad and Staithe behind you and The Maltsters over to the right, follow the small country lane left (Farm Lane) past an old barn and thatched cottage. Continue along the straight road for just under 500m up to a split. Ignore the track to the right and follow the Bridleway straight ahead and continue for about 200m further. At the split follow the Bridleway round to the right and continue to follow it for just under 1km as it skirts South Walsham Broad. Continue to follow the Bridleway round to the left, ignoring the private road on the right. Once at the road turn right and follow this back to the Staithe in Ranworth.

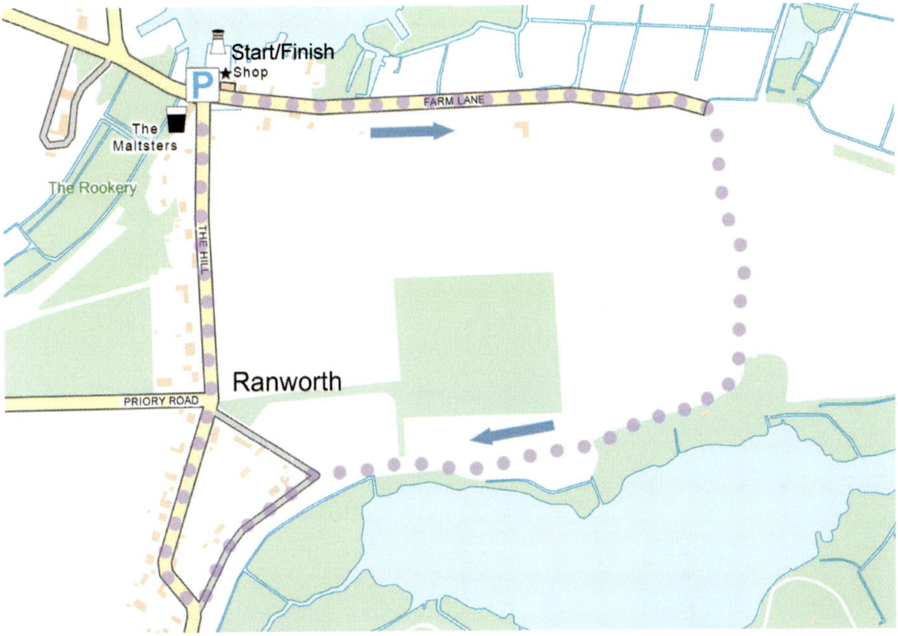

Salhouse

River Bure

Salhouse

Salhouse is a small village about 2 miles from the popular Broads destination of Wroxham. The village has a small tea room and The Bell Inn around a 20-30 minute walk from the quiet and secluded mooring on the south side of Salhouse Broad. Salhouse Broad mooring and parking is close to Woodforde's Brewery and the Fur and Feather Pub in Woodbastwick, with more information in the Woodbastwick Chapter. Boat Trips and Kayak hire are available from Salhouse Broad that allow access to Hoveton Great Broad nature trail which can only be accessed by boat. On the south side of the broad is also a campsite with views over the water making it one of the most tranquil places for an overnight stay.

Salhouse Broad

Salhouse Broad is a 32 acre privately owned broad with permissive access to the waters edge from the village and large area for mooring. The whole area, along with Hoveton Great Broad, Decoy Broad, and Wroxham Broad and rich with wildlife and the perfect place to sit and watch birds and dragonflies darting over the water.

Walk 31:
Salhouse Church

Distance: 6.5km (4.0 Miles)
Time: 2 Hours
Parking: Staithe Car Park **NR13 6RX**

From the moorings on the south side of Salhouse Broad follow the permissive path south away from the waters edge and after about half a mile the path arrives at a car park. Head out onto the road and turn right, following it for 250m and at the fork bear left along lower Street. The road passes the tea room and enters the village proper. If the plan is to visit the village pub then continue straight, if not then look out for a public footpath on the right opposite Thieves Lane. The path follows the edge of the paddocks and then along the field edge to a hedge line with a path left and right. Turn left here and follow the path along the hedge-line to All Saints Church. Once at the church, backtrack along the hedge-line and follow it to the north east past the path you walked earlier on the right and up to the road. Turn right and follow the lane up to the end of the road and then turn left back to the staithe car park. The permissive path will lead back to Salhouse Staithe.

All Saints Church, Salhouse
The lovely and secluded church of All Saints on the outskirts of Salhouse dates to the 14th Century and underwent some later rebuilding which was never completed.

Walk 32:
Woodfordes Brewery

Distance: 3.0km (1.9 Miles)
Time: 1 Hour
Parking: Staithe Car Park NR13 6RX

From the Mooring on the south side of Salhouse Broad follow the permissive path south away from the waters edge and after about half a mile the path arrives at a car park. Head out onto the road and turn left and follow the lane for 850m to The Fur and Feather Pub with Woodforde's Brewery just alongside. You can then retrace your steps back to Salhouse Car Park and to the staithe.

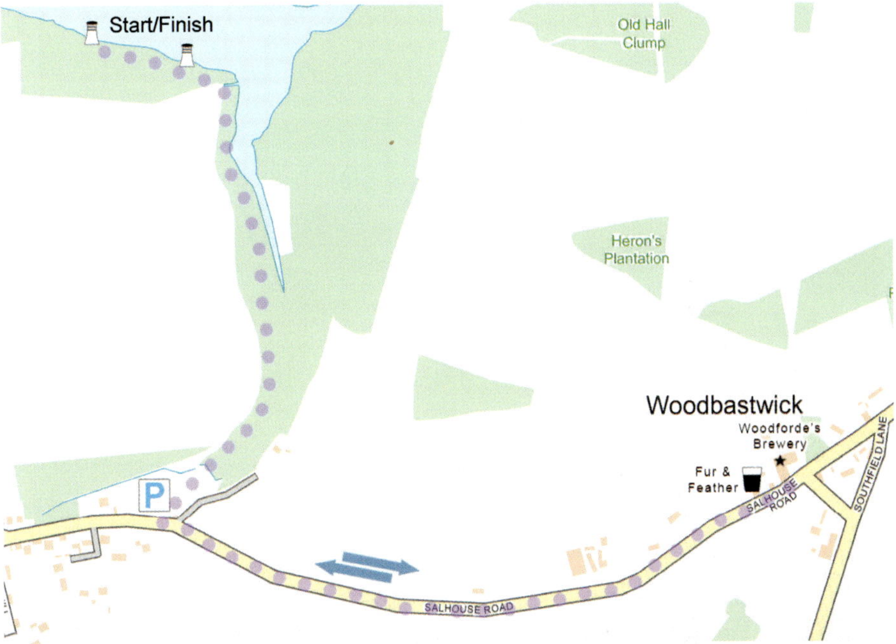

Somerton

River Thurne

Somerton

Somerton is a charming small village on the very north eastern edge of the Broads and at the end of the River Thurne. There are plenty of free moorings along Somerton Dyke with a small car park just at the end by the road. The Lion free-house is located just a 5 minute walk from the staithe and moorings and serves lunch and dinner 7 days a week through the holiday season. There are no shops or other amenities in the village, the closest being at Winterton or Martham just over a mile away. Somerton is also one of the closest points to the sea being just slightly further inland than nearby Horsey.

Somerton Staithe

Martham Broad Nature Reserve

Norfolk Wildlife Trust's Martham Broad Nature Reserve is a secluded wildlife haven, home to breeding Bitterns, Bearded Tits, Marsh Harriers and Cetti's Warblers. There is no access by road and can only be seen by boat or on foot from one of the footpaths that follows its southern or eastern side.

Walk 33:
Winterton Dunes

Distance: 9.2km (5.7 Miles)
Time: 3 Hours 15 Minutes
Parking: Staithe Car Park **NR29 4EB**

From the staithe head onto the road and turn right. Follow the road round to the left and at the next bend up ahead there is a public footpath on the left leading between houses to open fields. Follow the path across the field to the road and turn left and shortly ahead the path bends round to the right. At the fork keep right and after around 200m the path bends sharply to the right and heads south. At the next split by a large brick wall around Burnley Hall turn left and follow the wall to the east past the ruins of St Mary's Church in the woods on the right and onto the road. Follow the road straight ahead around Manor Farm with a sharp bend right then left and up to another bend with a track directly ahead. Proceed straight ahead to the east along the track. The track eventually turns into a minor road called Low Road and progresses up to a junction. Turn left and follow the road to the path that enters Winterton Dunes nature reserve and continue north through the dunes.

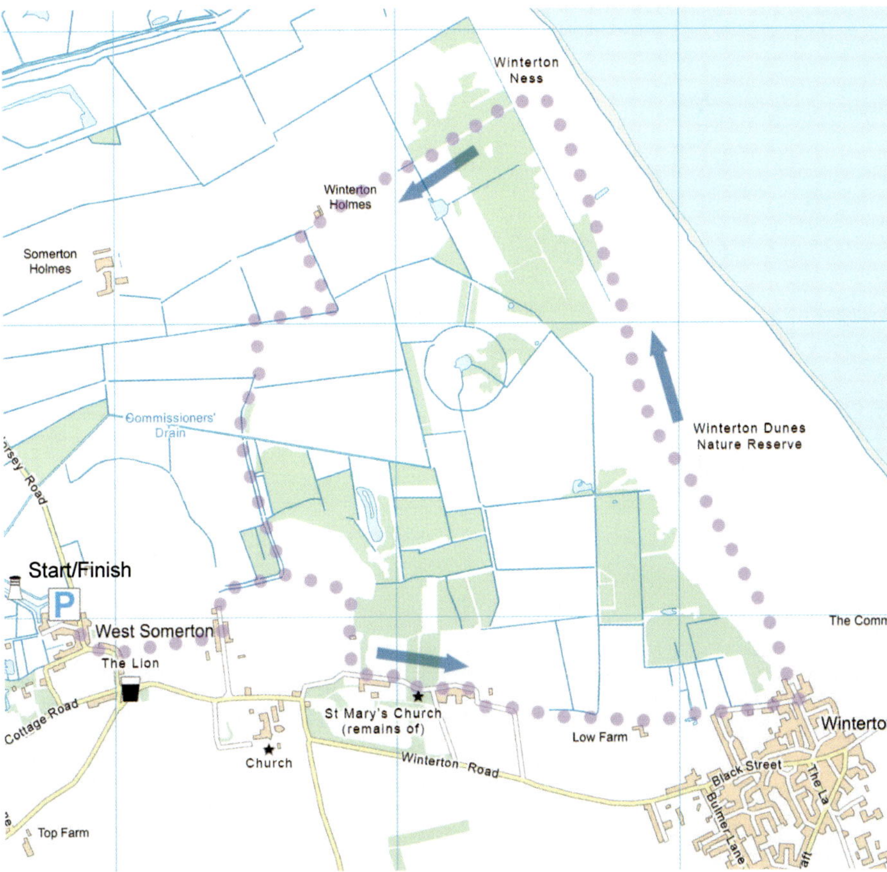

There is a massive network of paths around the dunes so make your way north until you reach the large concrete blocks that are Anti-Tank Defences from Word War 2. Head past the blocks and follow the straight track away from the sea to the west towards the farm buildings. Just past the large concrete pad and farm building the footpath bears left and heads south along the hedge line and then swings to the right and up to the farm track again. Turn left and follow the track south for 1km to the split in the track. Turn right and follow the track round to the left towards the houses, looking out for a footpath on the right that you followed earlier. Retrace your steps across the field and back to the road, turning right and following the road round to the right leads back to the staithe.

Winterton Dunes

Winterton Dunes is a vast nature reserve covering 109ha of beach, dune, grassland and woodland. The site is home to some rare wildlife including breeding Natterjack Toads and the UK's largest breeding colony of Little Terns.

Winterton Dunes

Walk 34:
Somerton Church

Distance: 4.1km (2.5 Miles)
Time: 1 Hour 30 Minutes
Parking: Staithe Car Park **NR29 4EB**

From the staithe head onto the road and turn right. Follow the road round to the left and at the next bend up ahead there is a public footpath on the left leading between houses to open fields. Follow the path across the field to the road and turn left and shortly ahead the path bends round to the right. At the fork keep right and after around 200m the path bends sharply to the right and heads south. At the next split by a large brick wall around Burnley Hall turn left and follow the wall to the east. Just as you enter the trees look out for the enigmatic remains of St Mary's Church ruins just on the right. Backtrack along the lane past Burnley Hall again and up to the road and bear left up to the sharp bend just ahead. Turn right down Collis Lane and after just a few metres there is a public footpath on the right through a paddock up to the church. Head to the opposite corner of the churchyard to arrive at Church Road and follow it until you reach the junction. Opposite to the right is a narrow lane, follow this north for just over 200m to a public footpath on the left. Follow this path along the field and back up to the road, turning right and following the road back to the staithe.

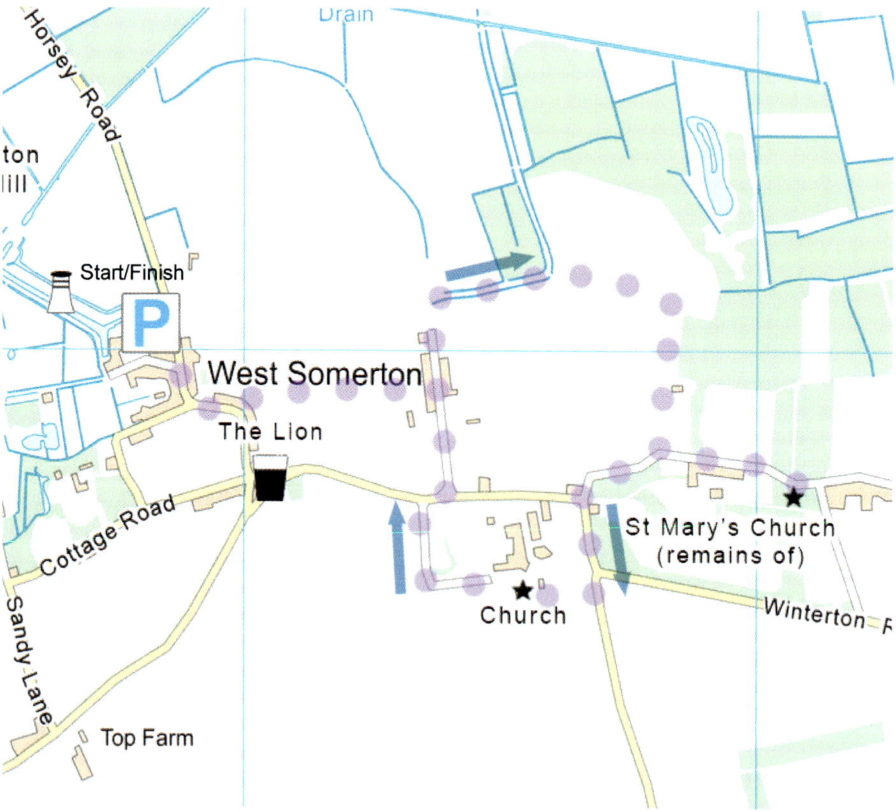

St Mary's Church Ruins

West Somerton is unusual in that it has two churches dedicated to St Mary, one of which lies in ruins in a small wood on the outskirts of the village. The Grade II listed ruins of St Mary's Church date to the 15th Century and is actually the newer of the two religious buildings but fell into disuse at some point in the 17th Century.

St Mary's Church, Somerton

St Mary's Church in Somerton is the oldest building in the village and dates back to 1200. The church underwent extensive restorations in 1867 and protected with a Grade II* listing.

Walk 35:
Martham Broad

Distance: 4.1km (2.5 Miles)
Time: 1 Hour 30 Minutes
Parking: Staithe Car Park **NR29 4EB**

From Somerton Staithe head onto the road, turn left and on the other side of the dyke is a footpath on the left. Follow the footpath along Somerton Dyke and past the moorings to a footbridge. Cross the bridge and continue along the riverbank path past West Somerton Drainage Mill and then along the edge of Martham Broad National Nature Reserve. After following the footpath round the northern edge of the reserve the path turns right and heads north along a dyke, gently curving round to the road. Once at the road turn right and follow it back to Somerton Staithe.

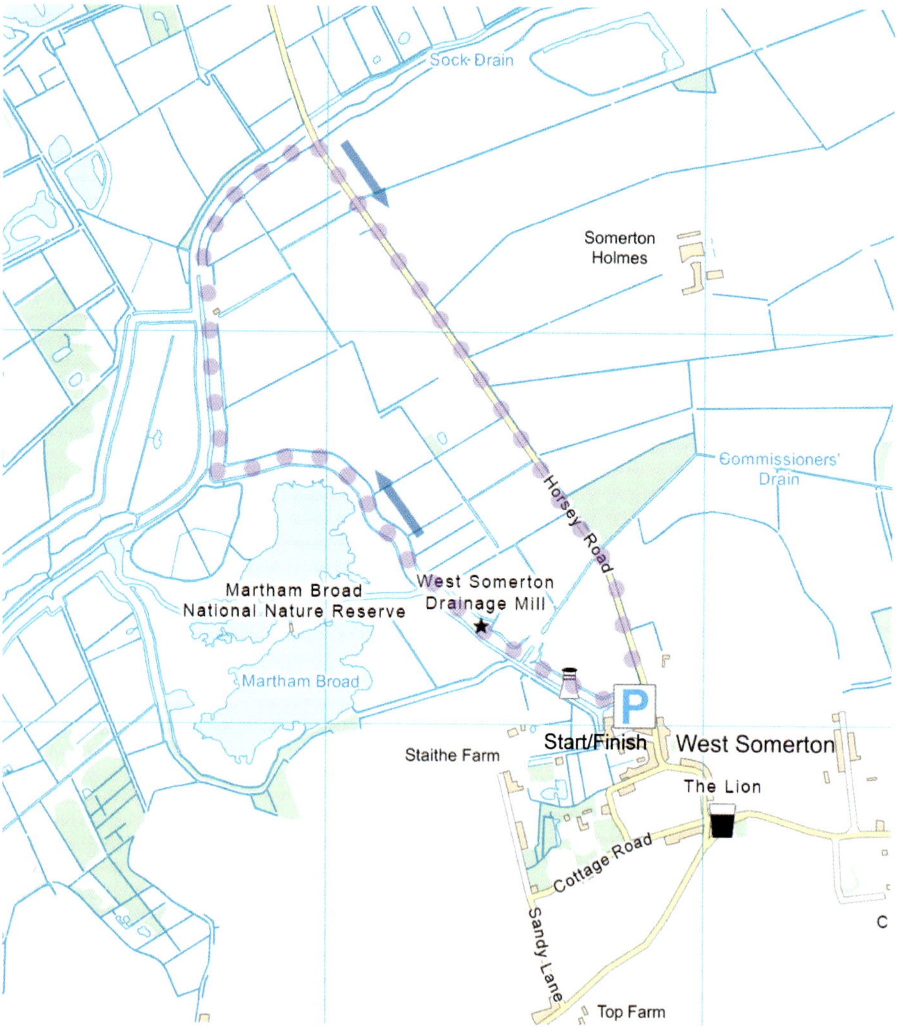

West Somerton Drainage Mill

West Somerton Marsh Drainage Mill sits along the access dyke to Somerton and dates back to 1900. The three storey tower has been given a Grade II listing and remains in good condition, complete with its internal workings.

South Walsham

River Bure

South Walsham

South Walsham is a lovely small village close to Ranworth and Acle and just below South Walsham Broad. Free mooring is available along Fleet Dyke, the access dyke to South Walsham Broad with a free car park by the access road to the moorings. The village is around a mile or so walk from the staithe and provides visitors with a pub and restaurant called The Ship Inn and the St Laurence's Centre for the Arts. Just on the edge of the village and bordering South Walsham Broad is Fairhaven Woodland and Water Gardens. This beautiful place provides a diverse and interesting habitat, with lovely walks to the broads edge. To the east is the Norfolk Wildlife Trust Upton Fen Nature Reserve with numerous permissive paths leading to a viewing platform overlooking the reedbed and broad.

St Mary and St Lawrence, South Walsham

Within the churchyard of St Mary is the ruined tower of St Lawrenc'se Church close to the St Lawrence Centre for the Arts. The tower, now only a fraction of its original height, has been made into a wildflower garden attracting bees and butterflies in abundance. The tower dates to the 15th Century and was sadly destroyed by fire in 1827.

Fairhaven Woodland and Water Gardens

Fairhaven Woodland and Water Gardens is a stunning visitor attraction, with a lovely cafe and adventurous walks along a network of narrow waterways through woodland to the edge of South Walsham Broad. Within its 131 acres grows some of the oldest trees in the area including a 950 year old Oak Tree which has stood the test of time. The woodlands and reedbed are alive with all manner of wildlife including dragonflies, butterflies and rare bird species.

South Walsham Broad

Walk 36:
Pilson Green

Distance: 4.5km (2.8 Miles)
Time: 1 Hour 30 Minutes
Parking: Staithe Car Park **NR13 6EB**

From the free moorings along Fleet Dyke, follow the footpath south in the direction of South Walsham. The footpath changes into a small road and arrives at a car park where you need to follow the track on the right just before it. This will pass behind the waterside thatched cottages and shortly turns into a road. Look out for the footpath on the right that passes through nearby fields and is sign posted to the village. After the walk across the field you will arrive at a road where you need to turn left and follow the lane past a small pond and telephone box and take the second country road on the left (Upton Road). At the end of the houses on the left, just before the national speed limit signs there is a public footpath. Follow this footpath in a straight line for 50m where it turns sharply left, continues for another 50m and turns sharply right. Look out for another footpath on the right after 120m. Follow this new footpath on the right all the way to the quiet country lane. On arrival at the road turn left and follow it for just under 1km. The road will turn into a track and pass alongside open marshes. From this trackway there are views over to Thurne Mill and the odd glimpse of St Benet's Abbey to the north. Look out for the large Oak Cross that marks the abbey altar.

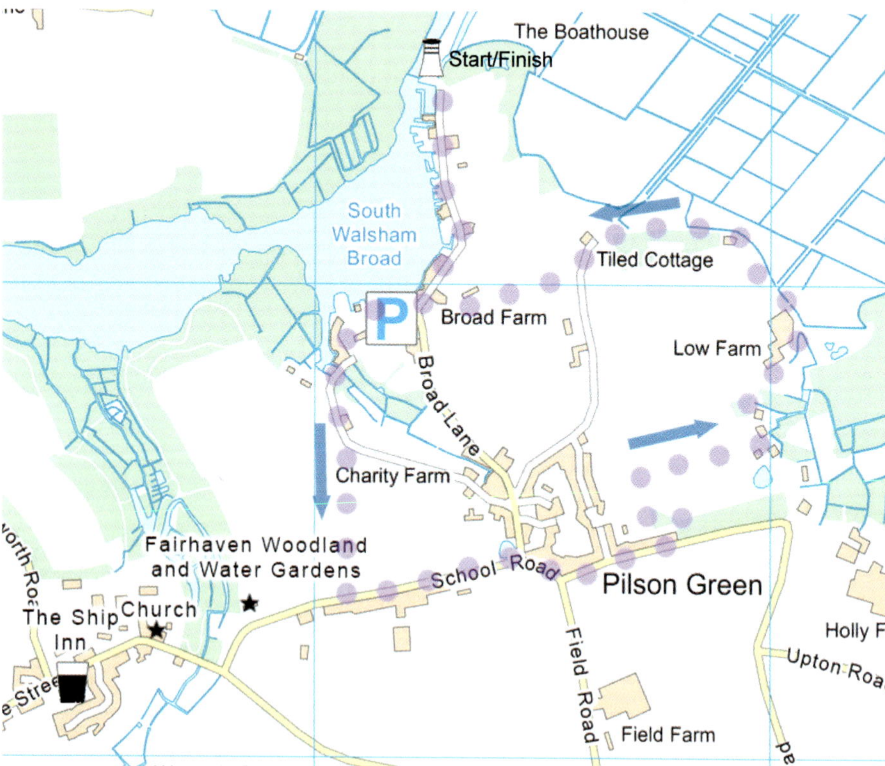

After the track joins another road turn left and look for the first footpath on the right after about 80m. This path passes alongside a field and gently ascents just a few metres above the marshes, but just enough to get a good view north. The path ends at the road just south of the car park. Turn right and follow the road to the car park or continue to follow the road to get back to the free mooring.

Pond at Pilson Green

Walk 37:
Upton Broad Reserve

Distance: 10.8km (6.7 Miles)
Time: 3 Hours 30 Minutes
Parking: Staithe Car Park **NR13 6EB**

From the free car park just near the broad, follow the road down Fleet Lane opposite the entrance. A path continues north at the end of the road and heads along the mooring area and along Fleet Dike. Continue past two further mooring locations until you reach the River Bure near the ruins of St Benet's Abbey. The remains of the abbey are on the other side of the river but look lovely from this point of view. Continue round to the right and along the River Bure past a small brick draining pump and up to the second pump about 650m away. Do not head through the gate just past the pump, instead on the right is a straight track that heads south, away from the river. Follow this track in a straight line until it turns to the left.

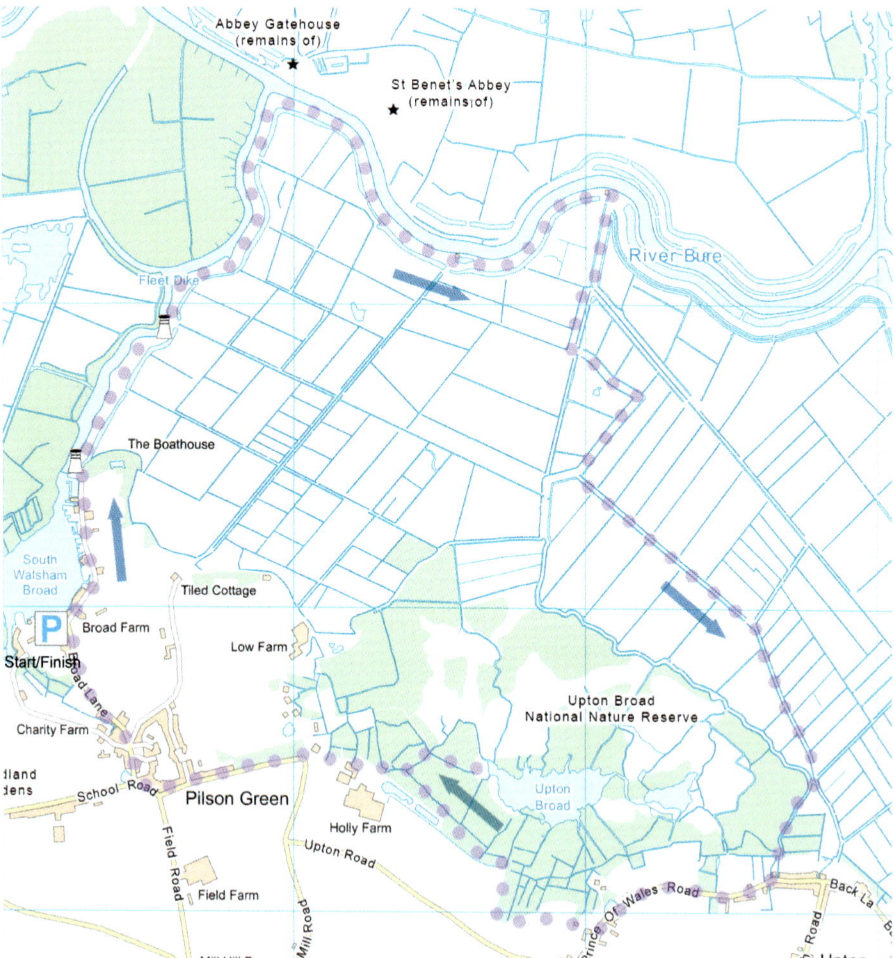

On the right at the bend in the track is a public footpath that follows a line of trees. Take this path and continue for 150m where you will arrive at a field – but do not go into the field. The path continues on the left for almost 300m and then bends sharply right for another 360m to a gate. Head through the gate and follow the wide path in a straight line for 750m until you reach a gate and the concrete road. Head onto the concrete road and turn right to follow it in a straight line for 580m and keep an eye out for a path on the right that heads over a bridge and through a gate. Follow this path up to the road. Turn right at the road and follow it for 700m to Cargate Green. Just past the driveway for Cargate Farm is a track that appears like a driveway but actually joins a public footpath. Follow this path past the horse paddocks and to a T-junction in the path. Turn right and follow this footpath in a straight line for 170m where it bends sharply left and heads along the edge of Upton Fen Nature Reserve. The route is surrounded by trees and a section follows a boardwalk to avoid the muddiest areas! Before leaving the reserve you will arrive at a gate with a sign showing permissive paths around the Fen. Head into the reserve for 150m, over a wooden bridge and turn right. Follow this path over another bridge and up to a small viewing platform. From here there are views east to Upton Broad and keep an eye out for the wildlife as there is much to see in this area.

Viewing Platform for Upton Broad

To continue the route head back along the same path and back to the gate which you gained entry to the reserve. Continue straight into Ivy Farm and then turn right to follow the road out. On arrival at the junction, turn left and then immediately right to follow the road into Pilson Green. At the end of the road turn right and then at the small pond, turn right again to follow the country lane back to the parking near the staithe.

Upton Broad

Upton Fen is a lovely secluded nature reserved owned and managed by Norfolk Wildlife Trust. Below is a map of the permissive paths through the reserve. These are subject to change and notices should be placed at the reserve entrances. **NR13 6EQ**

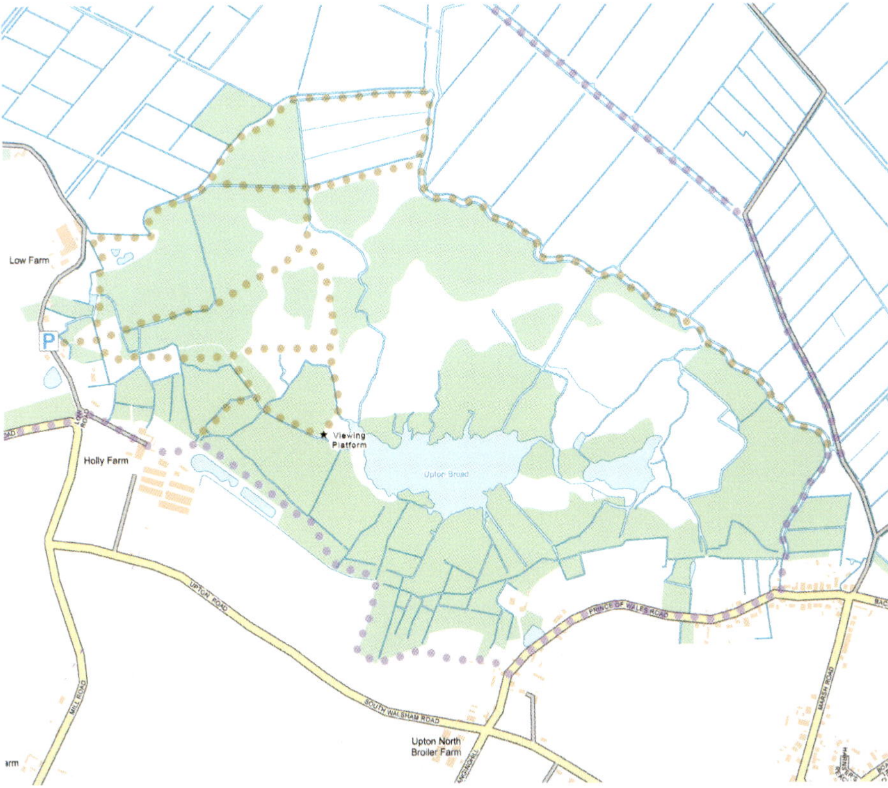

Grazing Marsh

Stalham

River Ant

Stalham

Stalham is a small market town that has grown vastly over the last few years. The town is divided by the A149 bypass with the staithe and boatyards on one side and the remainder of the town on the other. There are a fair amount of independent shops along the small high street with a large supermarket, takeaways and all other amenities you would expect of a town. Stalham has two museums, one in the town centre based at the Old Fire Station near the church and the Museum of the Broads, detailing the history and wildlife of the national park, located by the staithe.

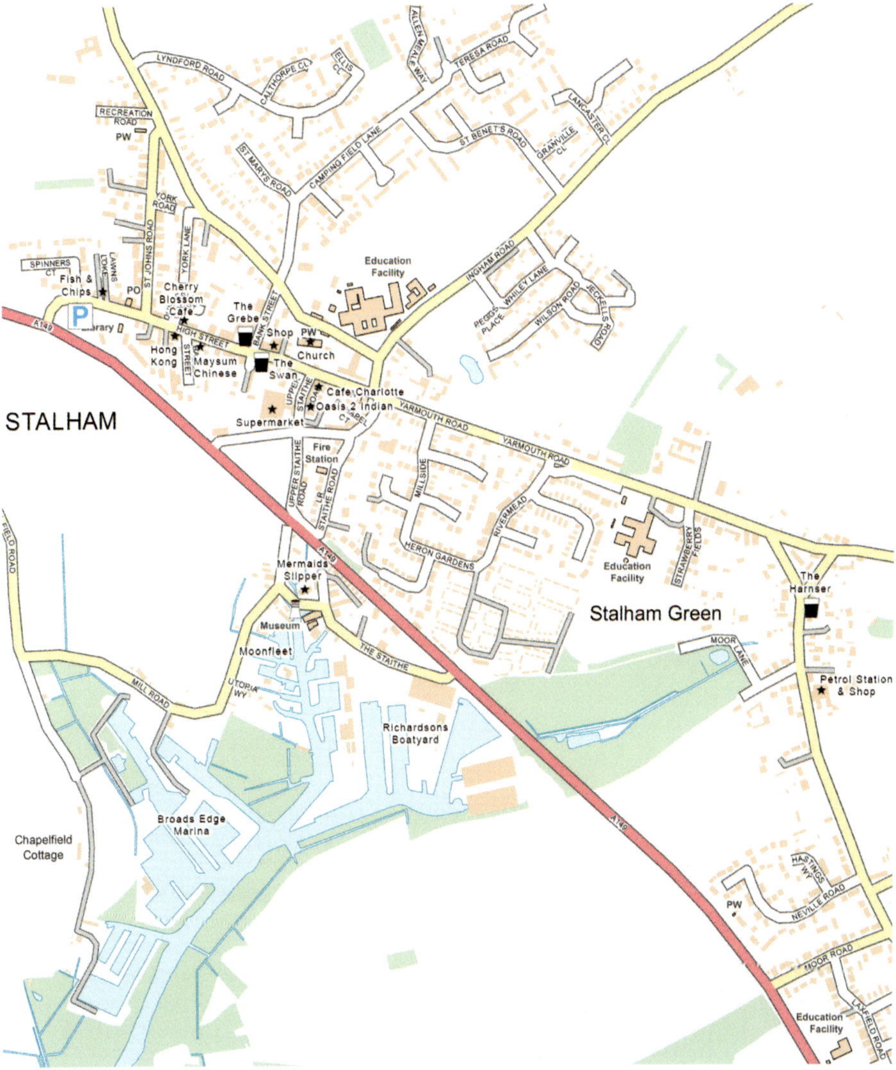

Museum of the Broads

The Museum of the Broads is located at Stalham Staithe and allows visitors to explore the history, wildlife and landscape of this extra special wetland area. Boat trips are also available along the River Ant from March to October on the boat called The Falcon, built in 1895.

St Mary's Church, Stalham

The parish church of St Mary lies in the centre of town and dates to the 14th Century. The church underwent extensive restorations in the mid 19th Century and given a Grade II* listing.

Walk 38:
Weavers' Way Linear

Distance: 8.0km (5.0 Miles)
Time: 3 Hours
Parking: High Street **NR12 9AH**

This is a linear walk along a section of the Weavers Way long distance path from Stalham to Bengate. Bengate has a fairly regular bus service back to Stalham but it is vital to check these times and plan accordingly. If arriving by car this walk can be started from the staithe (very limited parking) or from the large pay and display at the end of the High Street.

From Stalham Staithe, facing the Mermaids Slipper head left along the lane and just at the sharp bend at the end of the staithe turn right along a track signposted as Town Centre. The path heads up to a crossing of the A149 and on the other side joins Upper Staithe Road. Follow the road towards the large Tesco Supermarket and at the junction continue straight ahead along Upper Staithe road. The lane will arrive at the main high street, turn left and follow the High Street past the church and shops and almost up to the very end where it rejoins the A149 main road. Just before the A149 Main Road there is a footpath over to the right through a wooden gate and signposted as the Weavers Way. The path now follows the old railway line which once connected Stalham with North Walsham.

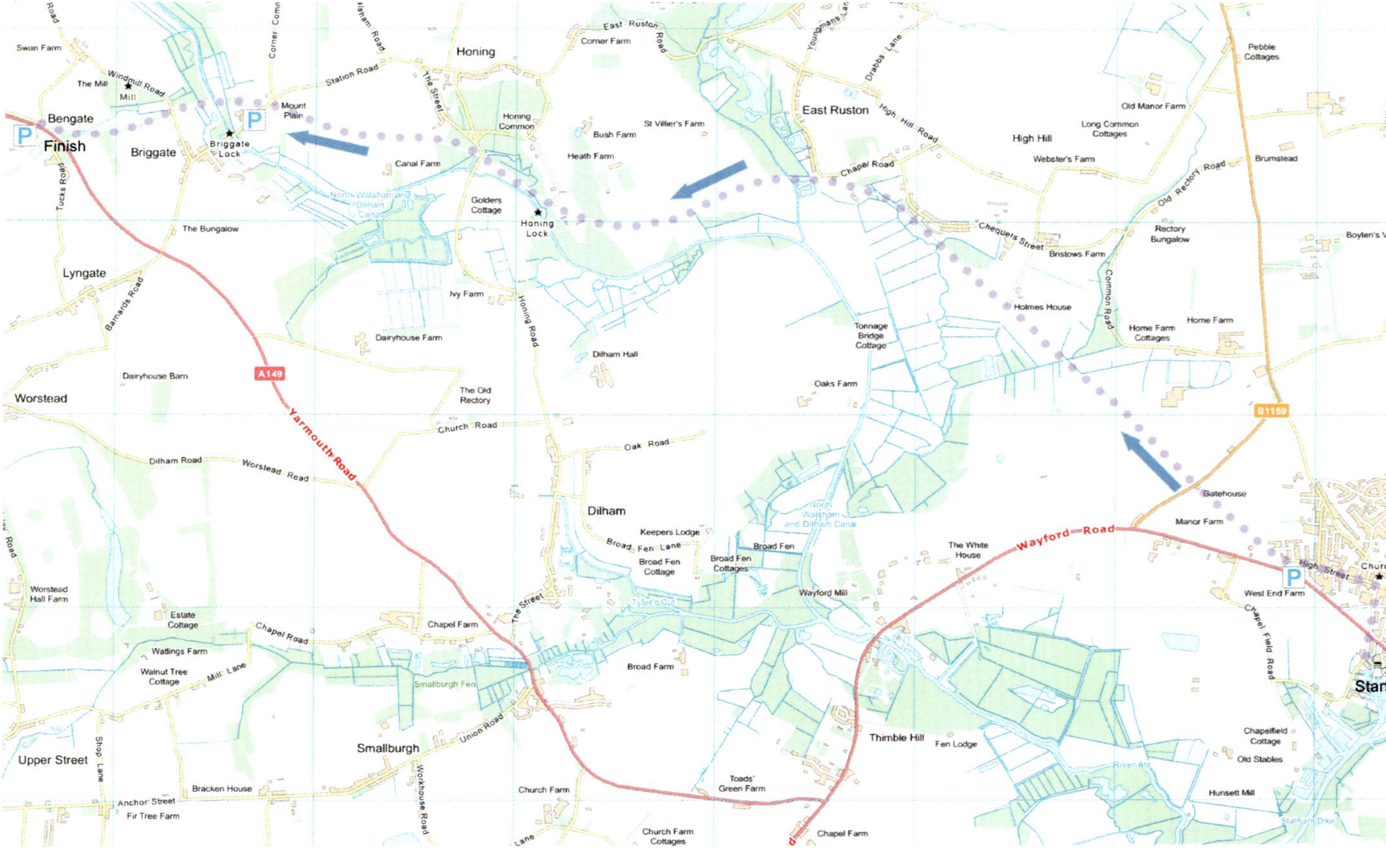

Finish
Start
Bengate
Briggate
Briggate Lock
Mount Plain
Honing
Honing Common
Honing Lock
East Ruston
High Hill
Lyngate
Worstead
Dilham
Smallburgh
Upper Street
Thimble Hill
Swan Farm
The Mill
Mill
Windmill Road
Corner Comn
Station Road
The Street
Corner Farm
East Ruston Road
Youngmans Lane
Drabbs Lane
High Hill Road
Pebble Cottages
Old Manor Farm
Long Common Cottages
Brumstead
Webster's Farm
Tucks Road
Canal Farm
Bush Farm
St Villier's Farm
Heath Farm
Chapel Road
Old Rectory Road
North Walsham and Dilham Canal
Golders Cottage
The Bungalow
Chequers Street
Rectory Bungalow
Boyten's View
Bristows Farm
Barnards Road
Ivy Farm
Honing Road
Holmes House
Common Road
Home Farm Cottages
Home Farm
Tonnage Bridge Cottage
Dairyhouse Farm
Dilham Hall
A149
Dairyhouse Barn
Oaks Farm
The Old Rectory
B1159
Yarmouth Road
Church Road
Oak Road
Dilham Road
Worstead Road
Gatehouse
Manor Farm
Keepers Lodge
Broad Fen Lane
Broad Fen
The White House
Wayford Road
Broad Fen Cottage
Broad Fen Cottages
High Street
Church
Worstead Hall Farm
Wayford Mill
West End Farm
Tyler's Cut
Estate Cottage
Chapel Road
Chapel Farm
The Street
Chapel Field Road
Watlings Farm
Walnut Tree Cottage
Mill Lane
Broad Farm
Smallburgh Fen
Union Road
Fen Lodge
Chapelfield Cottage
Old Stables
Shop Lane
Workhouse Road
River Ant
Toads' Green Farm
Bracken House
Church Farm
Hunsett Mill
Anchor Street
Fir Tree Farm
Church Farm Cottages
Chapel Farm
Stalham Dyke

After 600m the path crosses a minor road and continues opposite along the old railway line towards East Ruston. It's 2km along here before the route passes East Ruston and takes a gentle curve to the left in the direction of Honing. 1.6km further along the Weavers Way is a footpath on the left which is a detour to the lovely spot of Honing Lock. Take this detour as it is the perfect place to stop for a picnic! Return to the railway line and turn left, following it past a bridge and onto the village of Briggate with recent restorations and information boards for its once overgrown train station. Carry on along the railway path over a footbridge and across a minor road to reach Bengate and the A149 Main Road. The bus stop is just at the junction.

Briggate Station

Weavers' Way

The Weavers Way is a superb long distance trail linking the coastal towns of Cromer and Great Yarmouth, meandering its way through a large swathe of the Broads National Park. The 60 mile long route visits numerous pretty Norfolk villages and towns along the way including the old railway line here at Briggate, the Medieval bridge at Potter Heigham and Thurne Mill.

Walk 39:
Ingham Priory

Distance: 6.5km (4.0 Miles)
Time: 2 Hours
Parking: High Street **NR12 9AH**

From Stalham Staithe, facing the Mermaids Slipper head left along the lane and just at the sharp bend at the end of the staithe turn right along a track signposted as Town Centre. The path heads up to a crossing of the A149 and on the other side joins Upper Staithe Road. Follow the road towards the large Tesco Supermarket and at the junction continue straight ahead along Upper Staithe road. At the end of the road turn left to the church and then right, through the churchyard and out the other side onto the road. Turn left along the graveyard to Camping Field Lane on the right. Follow the lane for around 500m to a track on the left just after Allen Meale Way. Follow the track straight for about 50m and then round to the right. It will become a footpath behind the houses and then pass through fields and eventually arrive at the road. Turn left and follow the lane for only 100m to a footpath on the right along a line of trees. Follow the field edge path to the corner of the field where there are numerous paths heading off in all directions. You need to take the path directly ahead (east) which completes a couple of zig-zags along the edge of the field and arrives at the road by the pub and church. Turn right and follow the road past the church (Mill Road) for about 350m to a footpath on the right, opposite the village hall. Continue along the footpath through the fields until you reach Brick Kiln Lane and then turn left along the road until you find a footpath on the right just after Broadland Cattery.

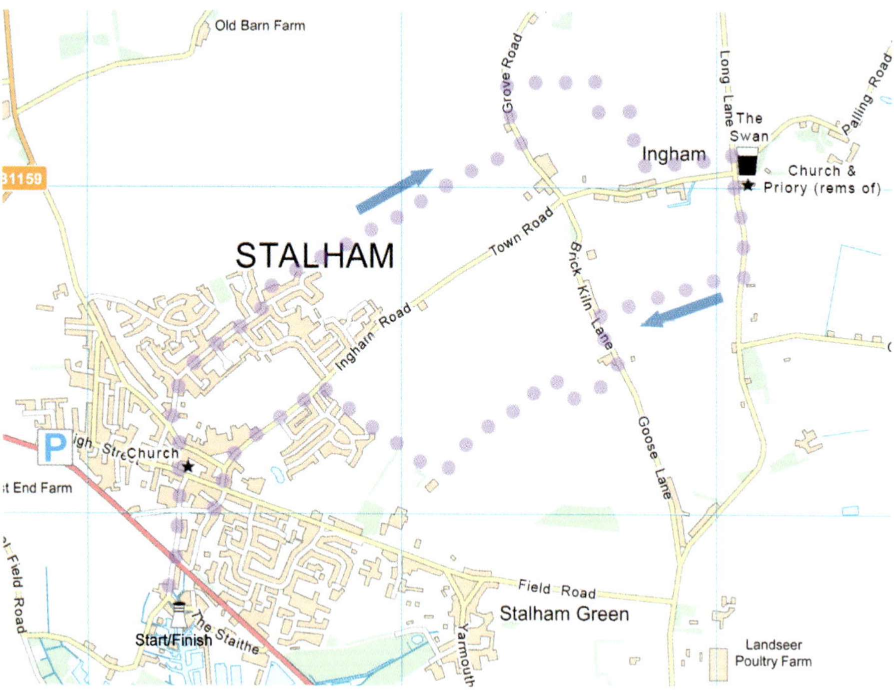

Take the path along the edge of the field, along a little zig-zag and then straight until you reach the farm track. Follow the track until you reach the farm buildings just ahead and then turn right just before the barn to follow the path around the building and along a field and housing estate to the road. Turn left and follow Ingham Road up to the mini roundabouts and cross to the other side along Lower Staithe Road. The road curves round towards Tesco Supermarket where you need to turn left along Upper Staithe Road and follow this back over the main road and to Stalham Staithe.

Ingham Priory

Ingham Priory was a Trinitarian Priory founded in 1198 with the present day church dating to 1340. On the church's northern side you can make out some of the original priory including a spiral staircase and numerous walls and arches.

Stokesby

River Bure

Stokesby

Stokesby is a remote village along the River Bure just east of Acle and the last opportunity to stop for boaters as they progress onto Great Yarmouth. A free car park by the staithe is available for visitors by car and plenty of free moorings close to the Ferry Inn. Attached to the Ferry Inn is the small village shop selling groceries as well as homemade savoury treats. The village offers some lovely walking with the parish church just to the east and paths along the riverbank in both directions leading to nearby disused mills.

Stokesby Staithe

The New Inn

Stokesby Mill

The mill in the centre of the village, known as Tretts Mill was built in 1826 to drive two pairs of stones and stands 4 storeys high. It is located close to the road making it an obvious feature when driving or walking through. The mill ceased operation in 1916 and given a Grade II listing.

Walk 40:
Muck Fleet

Distance: 7.3km (4.5 Miles)
Time: 2 Hours 30 Minutes
Parking: Staithe Car Park **NR29 3EX**

From the free car park and moorings just west of The Ferry Inn, follow the small track alongside the green to the country lane through the village. Follow the small lane opposite the green next to the village sign called Croft Hill. Keeping to the right, follow the footpath directly ahead ignoring the road as it bends left. This footpath will take you across an open field and then follow the edge for another 150m. The path will then follow a track as it turns right and shortly joins another track. Turn left and follow the track towards a farm but keep an eye out for the footpath before the farm on the right that takes you through the field. Take this path and follow it all the way to the country lane.

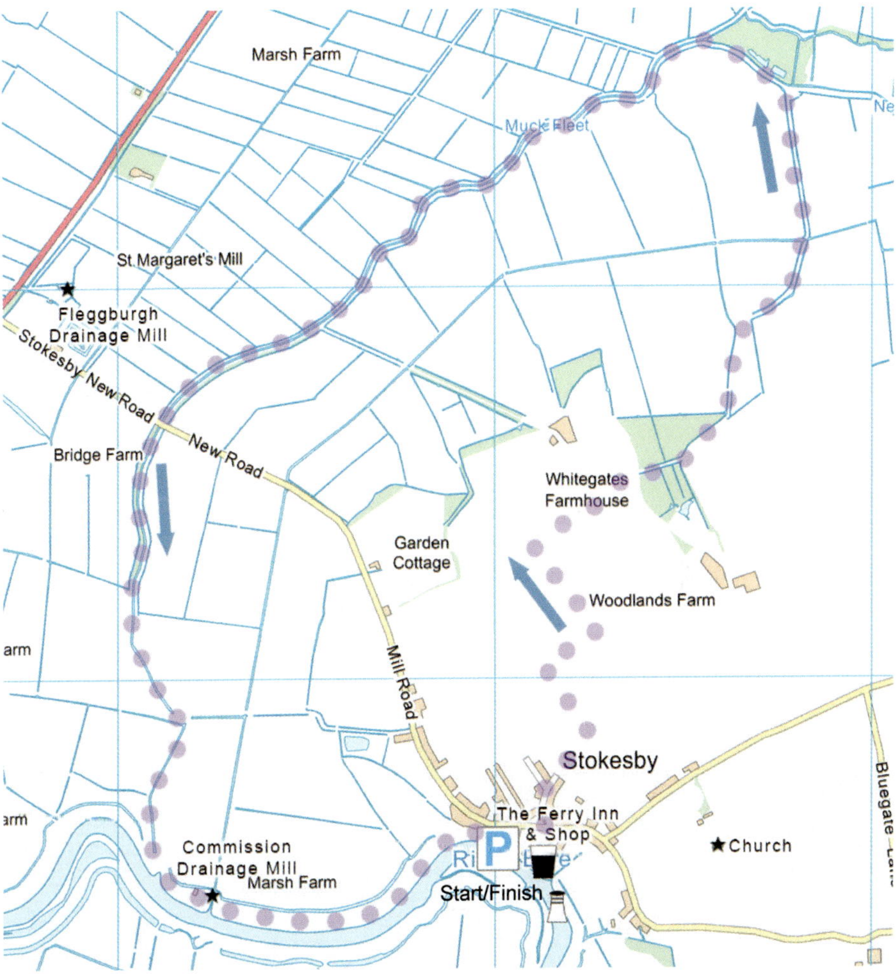

On arrival at the country lane, follow the trackway through the trees opposite. After around 550m there will be a fork in the track with the public footpath being on the right. Take the right fork and continue to follow the path along a raised bank as it curves north. At the first junction in the path turn left and follow the edge of Muck Fleet, over a wooden bridge to another trackway. Turn left down the trackway alongside Muck Fleet and continue for about 125m. At this point there will be a public footpath on the left just as the track swings right. Follow this footpath left which sticks to the edge of Muck Fleet as it meanders its way down to the River Bure further south. This is one of the prettiest sections of the walk with plenty of wildlife around and many wild flowers and plants.

Commission Drainage Mill

Over to the right you may see Fleggburgh Drainage Mill near the A1064 which is a lovely mill. Continue to follow this footpath along the dyke all the way to the road. Once you have reached the road, follow the footpath through the trees directly opposite. This path weaves its way through the dense foliage with a dyke on the left and open fields on the right. This section is superb during sunset with some fantastic views to the right. Eventually the path will arrive at a trackway leading left, right and straight ahead. Follow it straight ahead towards a pump station with the mill slightly to the left. At the pump station, follow the footpath up onto the bank and turn left. Continue to follow the footpath on the embankment all the way back to the village. The path passes directly under Commission Drainage Mill which is quite a sight and past a pretty cottage down on the left. Also on this path there are some lovely views to the left and right over the marshes and towards The Ferry Inn along the river. On arrival at the road turn right which will take you back to the Green and to the car park and moorings.

Commission Drainage Mill

Commission Mill is a disused drainage mill dating to the early 19th Century. The tower stands at 4 storeys high and has been given a Grade II listing.

Muck Fleet

Walk 41: Stokesby Church

Distance: 1.6km (1.0 Miles)
Time: 45 Minutes
Parking: Staithe Car Park **NR29 3EX**

From the free car park and moorings follow the small road towards the Ferry Inn. Continue to follow the waters edge footpath alongside some moorings and after about 150m from the Ferry Inn there is a footpath on the left. Take this path and follow it in a straight line to the road just ahead. On arrival at the road turn right and follow the country lane for about 280m and take the trackway on the left towards the church which is surrounded by trees. Follow the footpath on the right hand side of the church yard. Follow this field-side footpath all the way to the road. Turn left and follow the road to the junction and turn right. This last country lane will take you all the way back to the Green with the car park and moorings just over to the left.

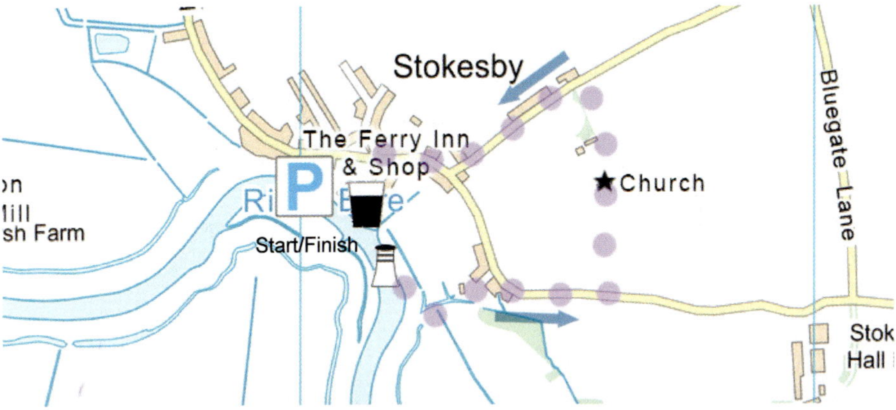

St Andrew's Church, Stokesby

The Grade II* listed church of St Andrew on the eastern side of the village appears slightly isolated from where the main settlement was established. According to the Domesday Book a church was present on the site but the current building dates to the 13th Century and went through restorations in 1856.

Walk 42:
River Bure

Distance: 8.9km (5.5 Miles)
Time: 3 Hours
Parking: Staithe Car Park **NR29 3EX**

From the car park at the staithe, follow the roadway out and back to the country lane through the village. Turn right and follow this country lane for 350m. The old school will be the last building on the right and stick to the road as it heads around the church which is up to the left in the trees. The road is followed for 2.4km from here until you reach the first lane on the right which is by Runham Church. Along this stretch of road there are lovely views down to the marshes on the right and stretching for miles into the distance. Also along here, where you arrive at Herringby Hall you may notice a stone wall, this is probably reused material from the demolition of St Ethelbert's Church and College that was once on the site as they look much older than the present hall. Turn right and follow the road past the church and to the point where it turns into a track and splits left and right. Follow the track to the right and after about 30m there is a footpath on the left. Follow this footpath through the gate into the open field. Follow the faint path through the field, over a small dirt bridge and to the metal gate on the other side. Pass through this gate and walk up onto the riverside embankment and turn right.

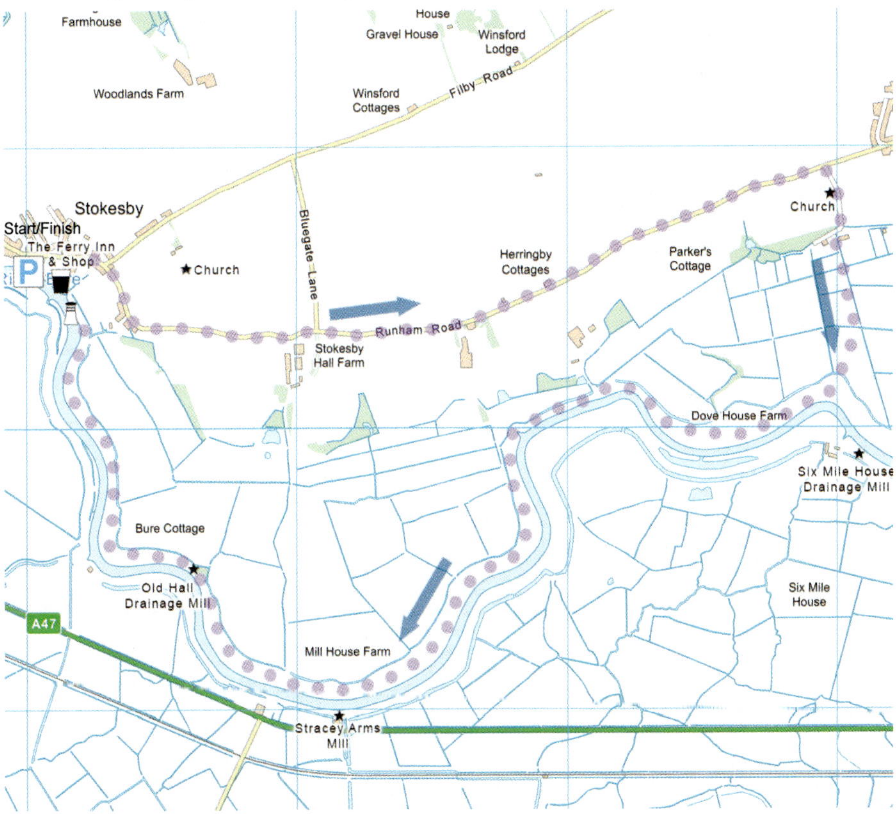

Pass through this wooden gate and continue to follow the riverside footpath all the way back to Stokesby which is nearly 5km away. Along this section you will pass through several gates near Stracey Arms Mill and Old Hall Drainage Mill. There are two doorways to the ruined mill and the millers cottage is just a stone's throw away. To continue the route, head back up onto the riverside bank and follow it to The Ferry Inn. Follow the footpath in front of The Ferry Inn and cottages back to the car park at the staithe.

Old Hall Drainage Mill

The small ruined mill along the River Bure is known as Stokesby Old Hall Drainage Mill and dates to the 19th Century, along with the nearby ruined marshman's cottage. The family that lived here would have taken care of the local livestock grazing the marshes as well as maintain the mill and ditches.

Sutton

River Ant

Sutton

Sutton is a small village that borders the nearby town of Stalham, on the northern end of the River Ant. The staithe is a popular stop for boaters, with Sutton Staithe Hotel offering a selection of food and drink throughout the day. In the village centre is a garden and aquatics centre and large campsite, with a pottery shop just on the outskirts to the east which is open during the week. Sutton Fen just on the south side of the village along the River Ant is a large RSPB Reserve which is sadly not open to the public. Just east of the village is Sutton Mill, one the tallest mills in the area.

St Michael's Church, Sutton

The Grade II* listed church of St Michael sits on the eastern most edge of the village on a slight hill which at the time of construction, would have overlooked the surrounding marsh and waterways. The church appears to date to the early 14th Century with restorations taking place in 1848.

Walk 43:
Sutton Mill

Distance: 3.9km (2.4 Miles)
Time: 1 Hour 30 Minutes
Parking: Staithe Car Park **NR12 9QS**

From Sutton Staithe head up to the main road and cross carefully, continuing down Staithe Road opposite. Follow the lane up to the junction by the pond and directly opposite is a footpath along a fence which follows a dyke and field gently round to the right and into the churchyard for St Michael. Join the road on the other side and turn right, taking the first lane on the left (Mill Road). Follow the lane for 650m to a public footpath on the left just by Sutton Mill. The path follows a driveway under the mill and north along a narrow path between fields. Once at the road turn left and follow Hall Road for 750m to the junction. Follow the road opposite to the left (Rectory Road) and at the junction turn left, heading south until you reach the small pond. Turn right here to follow the lane back to Sutton Staithe.

Sutton Corn Mill

Sutton Mill can be seen for miles around as it soars to 9 storeys above the surrounding countryside. Although unconfirmed it is potentially the tallest surviving mill in Norfolk but an official height has never been established. The Grade II* building was first constructed in 1789 at 8 storeys and had to be rebuilt in 1861 due to a fire, when builders added a ninth floor.

Walk 44:
Sutton Marshes

Distance: 4.2km (2.6 Miles)
Time: 1 Hour 30 Minutes
Parking: Staithe Car Park **NR12 9QS**

From Sutton Staithe walk up to the main road, cross carefully and continue along Staithe Road opposite. Take the first lane on the left (Laxfield road) and follow it to the junction and turn left up to the Main Road. Cross carefully and follow the footpath on the opposite side which follows the edge of woodland to the south west. The path skirts the edge of Sutton Broad and then passes through a couple of gates turning right to head north east with grazing fields on the right. The path follows the edge of woodland following a gentle arc to reach the southern edge of Richardson's Marina and then arrives at the Main Road. Cross carefully and follow the path opposite continuing to the road and following it straight ahead to Yarmouth Road (the main road through Stalham Green). Turn right past the petrol station and shop and follow Yarmouth Road south through the village and after 750m turn right down Staithe Road. Follow the lane and cross the main road to Sutton Staithe.

Footpaths through Sutton Fen

Thurne

River Thurne

Thurne

Thurne is a small village along one of the busiest stretches of river this side of Norfolk. The River Thurne alongside is a thoroughfare for boaters heading to Potter Heigham with Thurne Dyke being a popular overnight stop. The village has a small gift shop which also sells a few essentials, The Lion Inn, and a small car park by the staithe with plenty of moorings. At the end of the dyke is one of the most famous landmarks in the whole national park. The stunning white Thurne Mill sits close to the water's edge and it's likely you've seen the mill on dozens of postcards and book covers for the Broads.

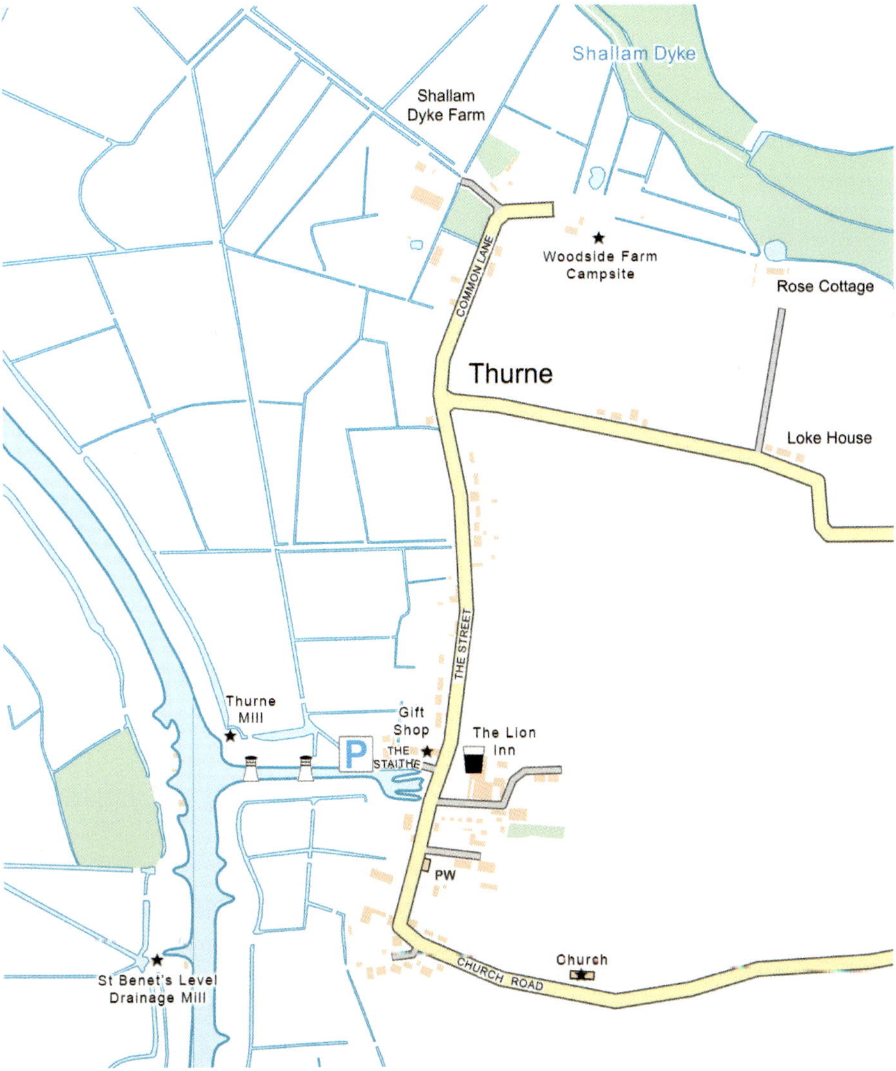

Thurne Mill

The stunning and iconic Grade II* listed Thurne Mill overlooks the nearby mooring dyke and rippling waters of the River Thurne. The mill is probably one of the most photographed in the Broads and dates back to 1820. On set days through the year the mill is open to see the mechanical working interior and observe the sails rotating.

Walk 45:
River Thurne & Oby

Distance: 5.4km (3.4 Miles)
Time: 2 Hours
Parking: Staithe Car Park **NR29 3BU**

From Thurne staithe follow the road away from the main river towards public toilets and turn right. Just opposite the toilets is a gate leading along a path on the south side of Thurne Dyke past moorings and round to the left. The path sticks close to the riverbank past St Benet's Level Drainage Mill (opposite bank) and eventually arrives at another dyke close to a holiday park. The path passes around the dyke and turns back to the River Thurne heading south and gently curves round to the left to South Oby Dyke. Follow the path to the end of the dyke and through the field, now on the Weavers Way, up to the track into Oby. Follow the track up to the road and turn left towards the farm, continuing along the Weavers Way around the farm and to the field edge on the other side which leads up to a track and access road to the holiday park. At the track turn left towards the entrance and just on the right the Weavers Way follows a zig-zag along the edge of the field to the church and road. Cross the road to the path opposite along the field edge and through the paddock onto the farm track and turn left, following the track through the farm to the road with the staithe opposite to the right.

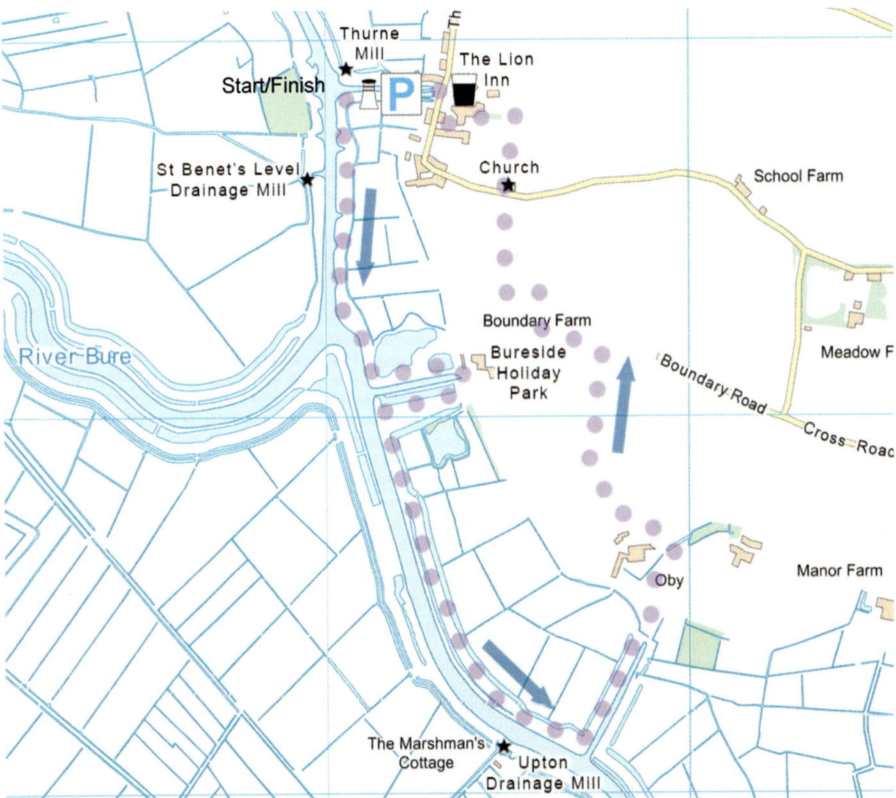

St Edmund's Church, Thurne

The small secluded church of St Edmund sits on the edge of the village and dates back to the 13th Century. The church underwent restorations in 1853 and has a selection of features and architecture dating from the Medieval period.

Walk 46:
River Thurne & Repps

Distance: 6.2km (3.9 Miles)
Time: 2 Hours 15 Minutes
Parking: Staithe Car Park **NR29 3BU**

From Thurne staithe head along the dyke towards Thurne Mill and join the riverbank footpath through the gate just on the other side of the mill. The path completes a long gentle curve along the River Thurne to eventually reach some waterside bungalows close to Repps Staithe. The path continues behind the properties and arrives at the road at Repps Staithe. Turn right and follow the road for about 600m, past Hall Farm looking out for a public footpath that crosses the road from left to right. At the footpath turn right heading south across the field towards woodland and pass through along the path to the other side. Bear right along the edge of the woodland to the west and once on the other side of the farm bear left following the path south west and up to the road. Opposite is a footpath that crosses the field diagonally to the right and up to the field edge. Turn left and follow the path south to the track and turn right towards the farm. Follow the track through the farm to the road with the staithe just opposite to the right.

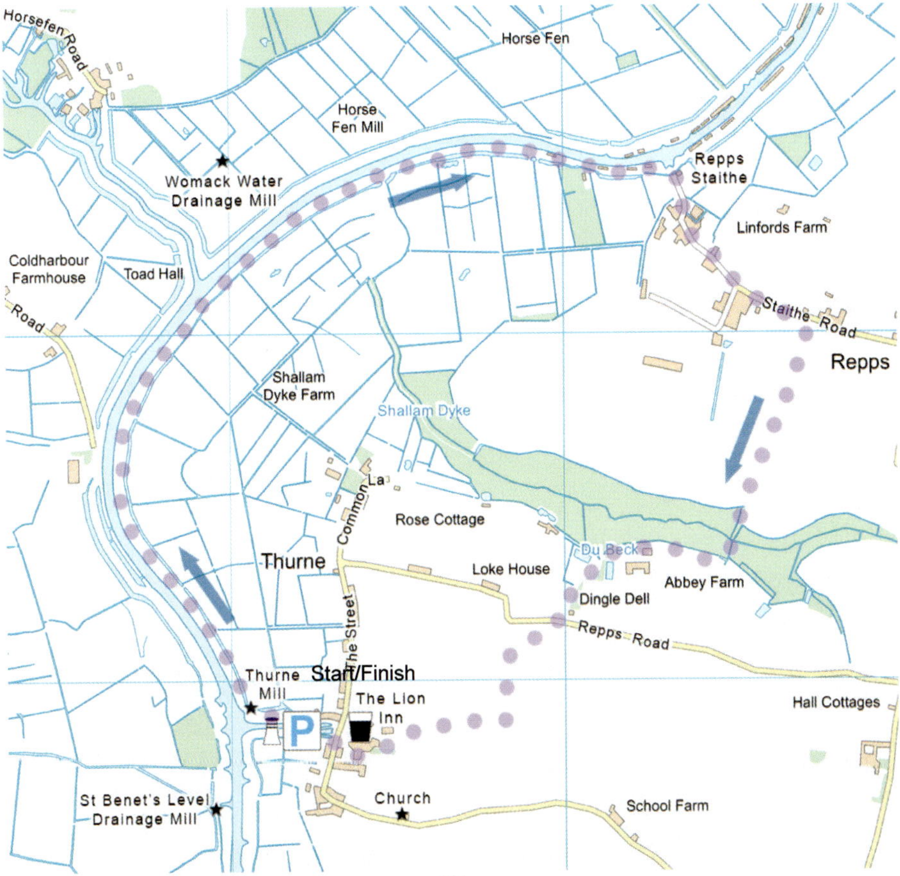

River Thrune at Repps Staithe

Upton

River Bure

Upton

Upton is a small village just a mile or so north of Acle and situated along the meandering River Bure. The staithe provides free mooring and parking for visitors with a short walk into the village centre to the local pub called the White Horse and small community shop which is open 7 days a week. Just to the north west of the village is Upton Nature Reserve, a wildlife rich area owned and managed by Norfolk Wildlife Trust with numerous trails through woodland and marsh. The site is best accessed from South Walsham and included in that chapter on page 149.

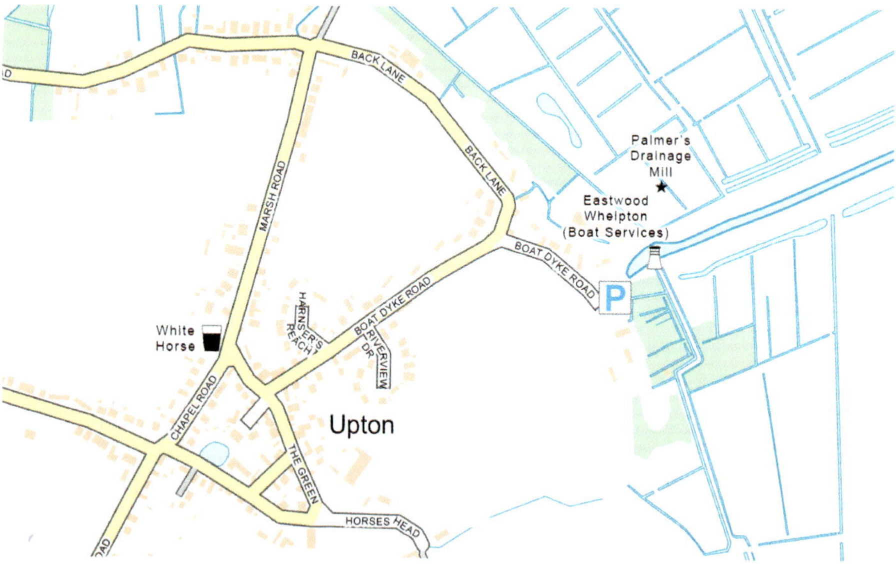

Upton Staithe

Palmers Drainage Mill

Palmers Drainage Mill sits alongside Upton Dyke and is one of only three hollow post wind-pumps on the Broads. The mill was built in 1900 and moved from its original site at Acle Marshes where it sat derelict and in danger of being lost forever. It has since been restored and remains a landmark for Upton Dyke.

Walk 47: River Bure

Distance: 3.8km (2.4 Miles)
Time: 1 Hour 30 Minutes
Parking: Staithe Car Park **NR13 6BL**

From Upton Staithe, join the riverbank path on the left side (north) of Upton Dyke. The path arrives at the River Bure and turns left towards Oby Drainage Mill on the other side of the river. The path gently curves round to reach Upton Drainage Mill where there is a path along a straight track on the left leading away from the river between the cottage and mill. Follow the straight track for just over 900m to a junction and turn left following the track gently round into the village of Upton arriving at the road. Turn left along Back Lane and after 350m the road bends round to the right and up to a junction. Turn left to follow the lane back to the staithe.

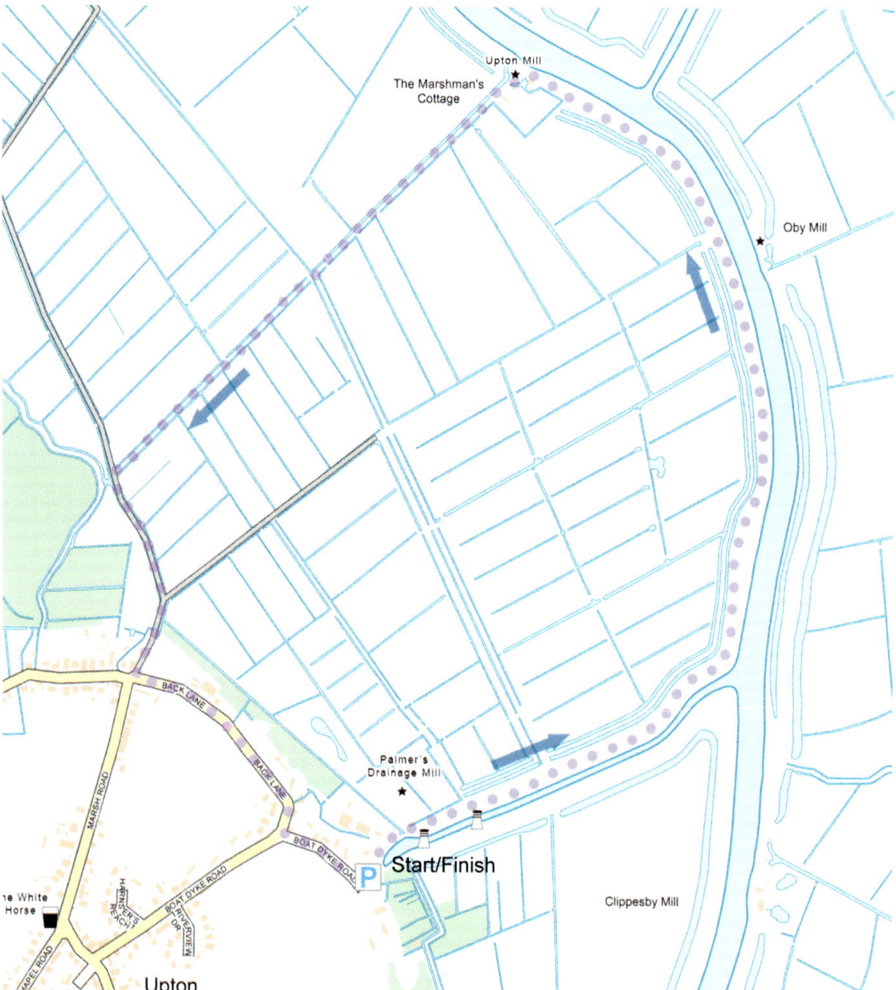

Upton Mill

Upton Mill, also known as Tall Mill is a large tapering tower mill dating to the early 19th Century. The mill stands at four storeys high and is made of tarred brick giving it a deep black look. Like many mills in the area it has been given a Grade II listing.

Wayford Bridge

River Ant

Wayford Bridge

Wayford Bridge marks the most northerly crossing of the River Ant and for some taller boats, is also the limit of navigation due to the low bridge. The Wayford Bridge Hotel sits right alongside providing overnight accommodation, bar and restaurant, with a large garden centre, cafe and farm shop just up the road selling fresh fruit and vegetables. A short walk along the main road will lead to the nearby petrol station and small convenience store. The marinas south of the bridge offer boat and canoe hire allowing visitors to explore the River Ant and also part of the lovely North Walsham and Dilham canal which is not open to motor cruisers.

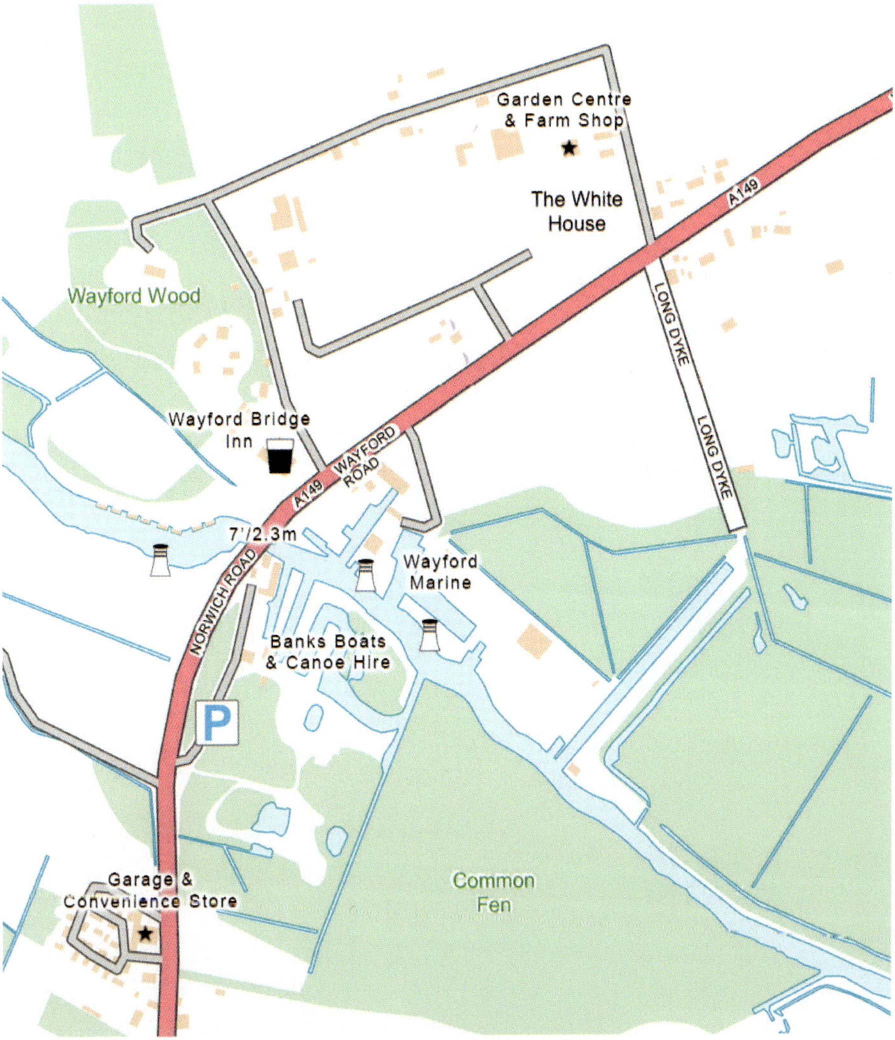

Wayford Bridge Moorings

Walk 48: Moy's Drainage Mill

Distance: 3.0km (1.9 Miles)
Time: 1 Hour
Parking: Roadside Parking **NR12 9LN**

From the moorings head up onto the A149 main road and turn right, following it south for just over 400m to a track on the right just before the petrol station. Head down this track for about 80m and turn left and continue until you join the field edge. The path follows the field edge south west to Low Street and once at the lane turn left and continue to the main road. Turn left and after just 50m there is a track on the opposite side of the road past Manor Farm. Follow the track north east to the end where the remains of Moy's Drainage Mill are located. Backtrack along the bridleway for just over 200m to a footpath on the right along a tree lined path up to the A149. Cross carefully and turn right back to Wayford Bridge.

Moy's Drainage Mill

Moy's Drainage Mill dates to the 19th Century and now sits as a sad remnant of what it once was. There's a tragic story associated with the mill about an 8 year old girl called Eveline who sadly died trying to save her little brother who had fallen into the pit of the drainage mill. Her younger brother survived until the age of 71 years with both being buried in Smallburgh church yard just down the road.

Woodbastwick

River Bure

Woodbastwick

Woodbastwick is a charming village with many thatched cottages spread out around the village green and stunning parish church. The Fur and Feather draws visitors from far around as it is one of the most attractive pubs in the area and serves a selection of drinks brewed next door at Woodforde's Brewery, itself offering brewery tours. The staithe and parking by the River Bure is around a mile from the village centre which also marks the entrance to Cockshoot Broad nature reserve, owned and managed by Norfolk Wildlife Trust.

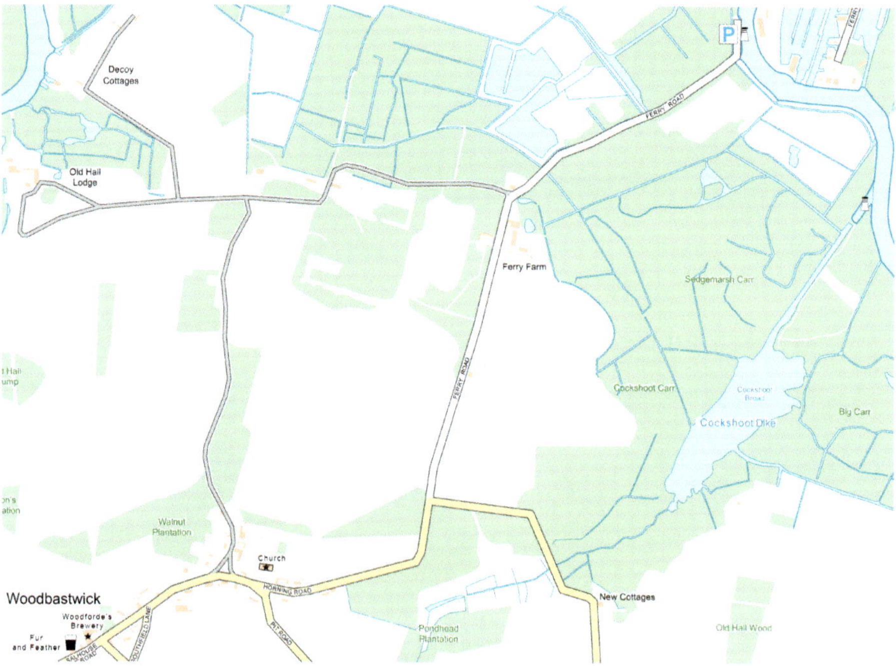

Woodforde's Brewery

Named after Parson Woodforde, a noted 18th Century Norfolk Clergyman, Woodforde's Brewery is an interesting place to visit. Visitors can see the famous Wherry Bitter being brewed and have a taste of it and other beers in the Fur & Feather just next door.

St Fabian and St Sebastian, Woodbastwick

The stunning church of St. Fabian and St. Sebastian is well worth a visit being just 25 minutes walk from the Staithe. The church was first built in the 14th Century and later restored in 1879. Most of the interior is Victorian but has some beautiful 13th Century wood carvings and has been given a Grade II* listing.

Walk 49:
Woodforde's Brewery

Distance: 4.9km (3.05 Miles)
Time: 1 Hour 30 Minutes
Parking: Staithe Car Park **NR13 6HN**

From Woodbastwick Staithe, follow Ferry Road away from the river and after just over 600m bear left, sticking to Ferry Road south towards the village. At the junction continue straight ahead, signposted to Salhouse and Wroxham and just ahead the road bends round to the right and up to the church of St Fabian and St Sebastian. Stick to the road as it gently curves to the left past the village green and up to Woodforde's Brewery and the Fur and Feather Inn just beyond. Retrace your steps back along the same roads to get back to the Staithe mooring and parking.

Although alternative tracks are shown on the map below please do not use these as they are private tracks with no public right of way. The only way to the village from the staithe is along the road.

Walk 50: Cockshoot Broad

Distance: 2.1km (1.3 Miles)
Time: 1 Hour
Parking: Staithe Car Park **NR13 6HN**

From the small car park alongside the moorings, look for the wooden bridge and entrance to the boardwalk just to the south by the information board. Follow this path alongside the River Bure for about 500m stopping occasionally at the viewing platforms for some great views up and down river. Eventually the path will arrive at another 24 hour free mooring area. Continue past the free mooring area, over a wooden bridge and turn right.

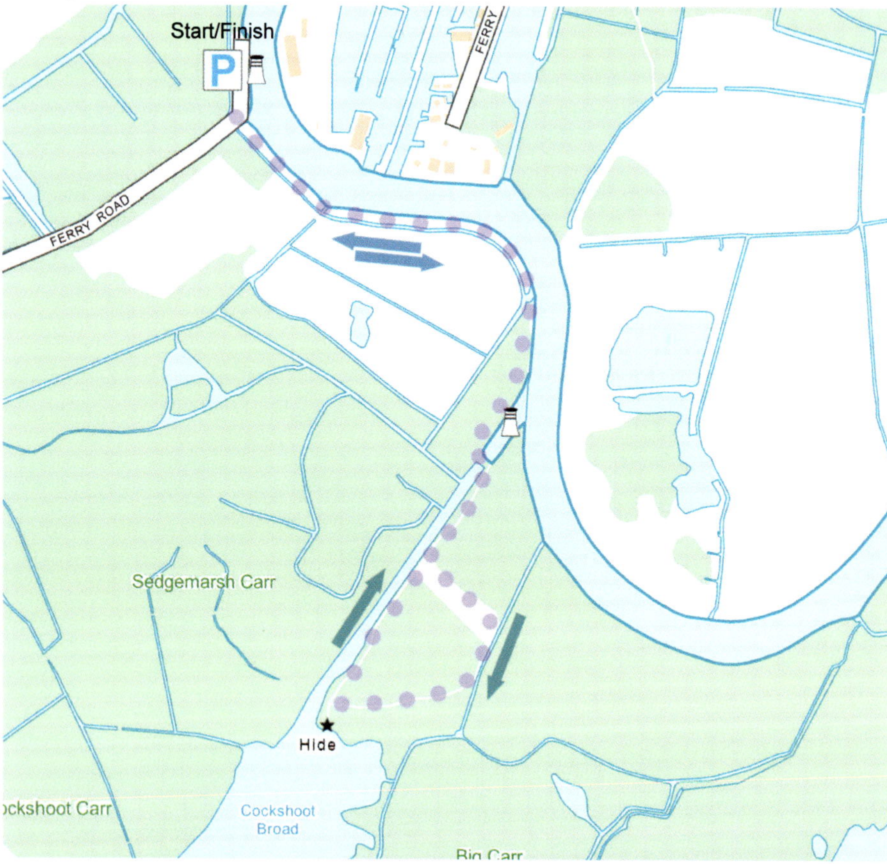

The route will follow a boardwalk alongside Cockshoot Dyke all the way to the bird hide at the northern tip of the Broad. Approximately half way down the Boardwalk is a turning to the left. Take this turn left and follow it through the reed beds and ancient woodlands to a junction and turn left again. This will take you to the bird hide for a short rest and spectacular views over the Broad. Follow the boardwalk back to the entrance of the reserve and retrace your steps back to Woodbastwick Staithe.

Cockshoot Broad

Wroxham

River Bure

Wroxham

Wroxham is a major boating and holiday destination, containing a majority of the pleasure cruisers on the Broads thanks to numerous marinas. The village, although usually referred to as Wroxham, is actually two separate parishes with Hoveton on the north side of the River Bure and Wroxham on the south side. Drawing in the visitors is the enjoyable riverside setting just moments away from department store shopping and multiple eateries. There's plenty to see and do in the village including taking a self drive boat out on the water, enjoying an organised trip exploring the local waterways or head out to the edge of the village and take in the tranquil surroundings of Hoveton Hall Gardens. A highlight for all animal lovers is Wroxham Barns, allowing visitors to feed the farm animals and browse several independent shops and galleries or enjoy lunch at the on-site cafe. The village is well equipped for the thousands that visit throughout the season, with large car parks, regular public transport links and one the the Broads Authorities Information Centres.

Wroxham Bridge

The original Wroxham Bridge lies under the current modern bridge to help protect the aging structure. The brickwork on the north western side is original and dates to 1619 with the entire bridge protected as a scheduled ancient monument.

Wroxham Barns

Wroxham Barns is one of the leading tourist attractions in the area, bringing in thousands of people to visit the craft shops and Junior Farm. There's plenty to see and do including a small funfair for young children, a mini-golf course, cafe and restaurant and a children's indoor play area.

Hoveton Hall Gardens

Hoveton Hall Estate and Gardens sits on the edge of the village and open to the public through the summer months with trails taking in the scenery and features of the grounds. The hall dates to 1809 and is protected as a Grade II listed building. It was constructed on the site of an older hall which was demolished just before the new hall was built.

Walk 51: Wroxham Church

Distance: 4.5km (2.8 Miles)
Time: 1 Hour 30 Minutes
Parking: Car Park **NR12 8UR**

From Wroxham Bridge, head over the new footbridge alongside past Broads Tours and along Norwich Road. Turn right along Church Lane leading over the railway line and to a sharp bend. Turning right here and bear left at the fork just ahead leads along St Mary's Close to the parish church. Backtrack to the junction and turn right heading south along Church Lane and after 300m follow the road round to the left over the railway again and to the junction ahead. Cross carefully and head down Park Road opposite and at the sharp bend ahead there is a public footpath just to the right in the trees. The path follows the woodland and arrives at an open field of which it follows the edge and progresses up to the road. Once at the road turn left and follow The Avenue round the gentle curve looking out for Staitheway Road on the right. Turn down Staitheway Road and after 200m there is a footpath on the left just after a private driveway which leads in a straight line back to the main road. Turn right and follow the main road back to Wroxham Bridge at the start of the walk.

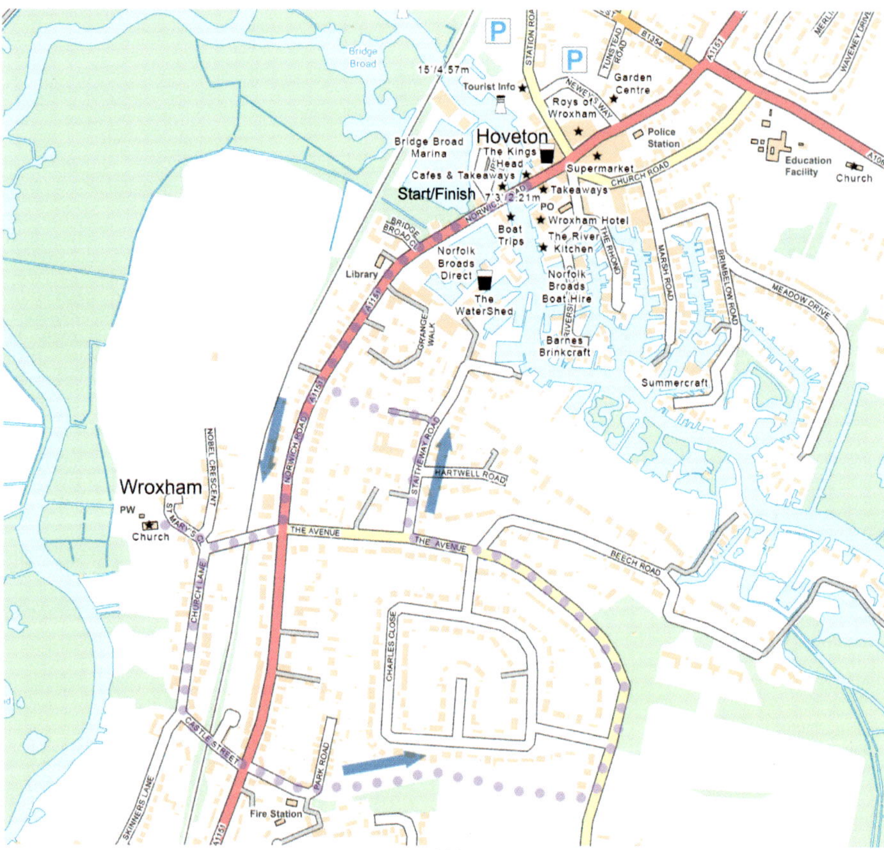

St Mary's Church, Wroxham

The lovely Grade I listed church of St Mary is set back from the busy streets and waterways and largely dates to the 15th Century. Within the nave are the remains of a 12th Century church which shows that the site has been worshiped on for nearly 900 years.

Appendix

Broads Authority
www.broads-authority.gov.uk

Broads National Park Information
www.visitthebroads.co.uk

Norfolk Broads Tourism Guide
www.norfolkbroads.com

Long Distance Walkers Association
www.ldwa.org.uk

Walking in the Wild
www.walkinginthewild.co.uk

Tour Norfolk Information
www.tournorfolk.co.uk

National Rail Enquiries
www.nationalrail.co.uk

Bus Timetables
www.bustimes.org

Other Books by this Author

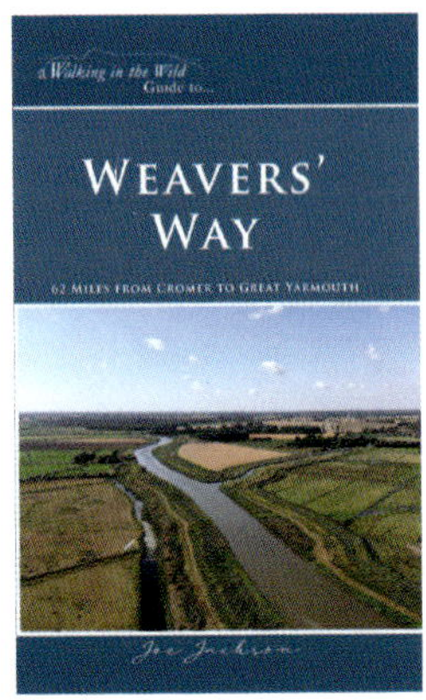